Data-Driven Healthcare

Wiley & SAS Business Series

The Wiley & SAS Business Series presents books that help senior-level managers with their critical management decisions.

Titles in the Wiley & SAS Business Series include:

Analytics in a Big Data World: The Essential Guide to Data Science and Its Applications by Bart Baesens

Bank Fraud: Using Technology to Combat Losses by Revathi Subramanian

Big Data Analytics: Turning Big Data into Big Money by Frank Ohlhorst

Big Data, Big Innovation: Enabling Competitive Differentiation through Business Analytics by Evan Stubbs

Business Analytics for Customer Intelligence by Gert Laursen

Business Intelligence Applied: Implementing an Effective Information and Communications Technology Infrastructure by Michael Gendron

Business Intelligence and the Cloud: Strategic Implementation Guide by Michael S. Gendron

Business Transformation: A Roadmap for Maximizing Organizational Insights by Aiman Zeid

Connecting Organizational Silos: Taking Knowledge Flow Management to the Next Level with Social Media by Frank Leistner

Data-Driven Healthcare: How Analytics and BI are Transforming the Industry by Laura Madsen

Delivering Business Analytics: Practical Guidelines for Best Practice by Evan Stubbs

Demand-Driven Forecasting: A Structured Approach to Forecasting, Second Edition by Charles Chase

Demand-Driven Inventory Optimization and Replenishment: Creating a More Efficient Supply Chain by Robert A. Davis

Developing Human Capital: Using Analytics to Plan and Optimize Your Learning and Development Investments by Gene Pease, Barbara Beresford, and Lew Walker

Economic and Business Forecasting: Analyzing and Interpreting Econometric Results by John Silvia, Azhar Iqbal, Kaylyn Swankoski, Sarah Watt, and Sam Bullard

The Executive's Guide to Enterprise Social Media Strategy: How Social Networks Are Radically Transforming Your Business by David Thomas and Mike Barlow

Foreign Currency Financial Reporting from Euros to Yen to Yuan: A Guide to Fundamental Concepts and Practical Applications by Robert Rowan

Harness Oil and Gas Big Data with Analytics: Optimize Exploration and Production with Data-Driven Models by Keith Holdaway

Health Analytics: Gaining the Insights to Transform Health Care by Jason Burke

Heuristics in Analytics: A Practical Perspective of What Influences Our Analytical World by Carlos Andre Reis Pinheiro and Fiona McNeill

Human Capital Analytics: How to Harness the Potential of Your Organization's Greatest Asset by Gene Pease, Boyce Byerly, and Jac Fitz-enz

Implement, Improve and Expand Your Statewide Longitudinal Data System: Creating a Culture of Data in Education by Jamie McQuiggan and Armistead Sapp

Killer Analytics: Top 20 Metrics Missing from Your Balance Sheet by Mark Brown

Predictive Analytics for Human Resources by Jac Fitz-enz and John Mattox II

Predictive Business Analytics: Forward-Looking Capabilities to Improve Business Performance by Lawrence Maisel and Gary Cokins

Retail Analytics: The Secret Weapon by Emmett Cox

Social Network Analysis in Telecommunications by Carlos Andre Reis Pinheiro

Statistical Thinking: Improving Business Performance, Second Edition by Roger W. Hoerl and Ronald D. Snee

Taming the Big Data Tidal Wave: Finding Opportunities in Huge Data Streams with Advanced Analytics by Bill Franks

Too Big to Ignore: The Business Case for Big Data by Phil Simon

Using Big Data Analytics: Turning Big Data into Big Money by Jared Dean

The Value of Business Analytics: Identifying the Path to Profitability by Evan Stubbs

The Visual Organization: Data Visualization, Big Data, and the Quest for Better Decisions by Phil Simon

Win with Advanced Business Analytics: Creating Business Value from Your Data by Jean Paul Isson and Jesse Harriott

For more information on any of the above titles, please visit www.wiley.com.

Data-Driven Healthcare

How Analytics and BI are
Transforming the Industry

Laura Madsen

WILEY

Library of Congress Cataloging-in-Publication Data:

ISBN 9781118772218 (Hardcover)
ISBN 9781118973882 (ePDF)
ISBN 9781118973899 (ePub)

Printed in the United States of America

10 9 8 7 6 5 4 3 2 1

To my father

Contents

Foreword

Healthcare is in a disruptive phase as it reinvents itself. The globally noncompetitive cost of the U.S. healthcare system (18 percent of gross domestic product) has forced significant and immediate cost reduction pressures onto providers. New clinical technologies continue to be invented, but their application lags. Quality of care and patient experience data is now widely available on government and private websites. Providers are moving from fee-for-service revenue to value-based purchasing systems. And because of the Affordable Care Act, new organizational structures and relationships are emerging.

In this chaotic environment, the effective use data is a potential path forward to success. The groundwork has been laid with the HITECH Act of 2009, as it provided the funding for the broad application of new information technologies into the care delivery system of the United States.

However, the opportunity presented by these new data resources has not yet been achieved.

To succeed over the long term, healthcare organizations need to move from merely collecting data to becoming data driven.

Laura Madsen provides a comprehensive plan for becoming a data-driven organization in this book as she outlines the current state of healthcare data use and its potential to transform an organization. She builds on the concepts in her first book—*Healthcare Business Intelligence*—to provide the steps needed to embrace the new opportunities for an organization to use data for strategy development and operational improvement.

Senior managers are now demanding more actionable and strategic information from their extensive investment in these new technologies. They demand information that can be used to solve problems and implement strategy. Multiple vendors now offer "solutions," and the lure of big data beckons. However, Madsen moves beyond the hype and confronts this new reality with a practical approach—RISE:

Reduce the unknowns in your data.

Identify the alternatives for analytics and storage and test them.

Standardize the data through effective data governance.

Evaluate and improve all aspects of the program continuously.

She also provides useful a set of actions that can improve data warehousing, use big data systems effectively, make data useful to decision makers, and manage privacy and confidentiality issues.

A data-driven healthcare organization will meets its community's needs and compete effectively. Once the structure of the program is in place, data-driven organizations can use their data assets to address issues such as:

- Predictive analysis of patient readmissions.
- Chronic disease management.
- Emergency Department over use.
- Revenue cycle optimization.
- Population health trends for selected patient groups.
- Patient complaint analysis.
- Privacy and security monitoring of clinical information systems.
- Out-of-network utilization for accountable care organizations.
- Clinical research on drug efficacy and cost.
- Demographic research for locations of new facilities.

All of these strategic and operational issues can be effectively addressed if the organization is data driven.

Other industries have embraced information technology, and these tools have radically restructured financial services, retailing, and manufacturing. Healthcare is beginning this journey, and the implementation of the electronic health record is only the first step. This is not easy work, and achieving a data-driven organization requires leadership and discipline. Laura Madsen provides the roadmap to success for the data-driven healthcare organization of the future.

Daniel B. McLaughlin
Director, Center for Health and Medical Affairs
University of St. Thomas, Minneapolis, Minnesota

For the Skimmers

I'm on an airplane right now, and there's a gentleman in front of me who is paging through a book, marking the pages that he wants to (presumably) go back to. It occurred to me that someone might do that with this book. Truth be told, I'm a skimmer. I love books; right now I have five on my bedside table and four on the floor next to it (the "read" pile). But certain titles encourage skimming more than others, and who am I to judge? So, for those of you in mind, here are the chapters quips, and outtakes that I think are the most useful to tune into. In reality, the whole book is great, chock-full of humor and insight, so if you're up for it, read the pages in between, too.

- In Chapter 1, read the section *"Data* Is a Four-Letter Word" to see how SWOTs can help you decide whether you want to move forward.
- Chapter 2 discusses "What Is 'Data Driven,' and Why Does It Matter?"
- Also in Chapter 2, because it's the foundation for much of the content in the book, read the section titled "RISE."
- All of Chapter 3 is important, but if you need to focus, start at "Data Is *Your* Asset—Manage It That Way."
- Chapter 4 outlines the ways to leapfrog BI maturity; start at "Hadoop, the Cloud, and Modern Data Platforms" and then go back and read the rest.
- Chapter 5 is required reading.
- Chapter 6 talks about "big data"—a topic that is admittedly not on the top of my list, but check out the section titled "Evolve or Die."

■ Chapter 7 addresses the need to make data consumable; read the section called "Why Do We Want to Visually Represent Our Data?"

■ Chapter 8 sections to review are "Barriers Are Everywhere" and "Process and Technology."

■ Finally, Chapter 9 should be read in its entirety. It's the culmination of the entire book and outlines what to do the first year of your data-driven journey.

Happy reading!

Acknowledgments

There are so many people to thank who have provided support and encouragement, their time, and input that it's almost too many names to write down. I would like to thank my clients, who have placed their trust in me to help them on this journey. It has been an honor and a privilege.

I must thank Lancet Data Sciences, an organization of wildly bright people who have dedicated their time to advancing the maturity of business intelligence across all industries. Many of my coworkers have provided support in the form of brainstorming, discussions, and content recommendations. They include (but are not limited to) Harold Richter, Paul Sorenson, Jesse McElmury, Mike Erickson, Rachel Urbanowicz, Chad Burgeson, Jennifer Mannhardt, Steve Boos (for that kick-butt Appendix D), Andy Holtan, and Tom Niccum. A big "thanks" goes to Cindy Alewine and Justine Messer for being great cheerleaders. I will be forever grateful to the rest of the organization for their support and encouragement.

The people who deserve most of my gratitude and appreciation are my family for their love, support, and patience. Even when they asked me, "How's the book going?" and I'd answer with a roll of my eyes, it meant a lot to me that they were interested and supportive. My biggest "thank you" goes to my husband, Karl, and my son, Nolan, for their patience above all. It's a big commitment, not just from me, but from my family, to write a book. They deserve as much recognition as I do.

CHAPTER 1

What Does Data Mean to You?

DATA:

noun plural but singular or plural in construction, often attributive \dā-tə, ʻda-*also* ʻdä-\

1. Factual information (as measurements or statistics) used as a basis for reasoning, discussion, or calculation. <the *data* is plentiful and easily available—H. A. Gleason, Jr.><comprehensive *data* on economic growth have been published—N. H. Jacoby>
2. Information output by a sensing device or organ that includes both useful and irrelevant or redundant information and must be processed to be meaningful.
3. Information in numerical form that can be digitally transmitted or processed.

(Merriam-Webster, 2014)

The frenetic pace of change in healthcare has been hard to deal with. The broad adoption of electronic health records (EHRs) has ushered in a wave of data that most organizations are not sure what to do with, beyond the standard regulatory reporting. The HITECH Act of 2009 ensured that data, for all the good and bad, is here to stay. Everyone wants it, but very few organizations really know how to get it or what to do with it once it's there.

When I work with organizations that are just getting started, they often express similar concerns:

- "Where do I start?"
- "Do I have the right staff?"
- "Do I have the right technology?"
- "What are other healthcare organizations doing?"

The answers to those questions are easy compared to the next question: "How?" How do you start? How do you know you have the right staff or technology, and how (and perhaps more important, why) would you compare yourself to other healthcare organizations?

Today, it's a forgone conclusion that we have to manage our data. Not just because we have so much of it but because there is so much assumed value in the data. The challenge is that the pace of change is so rapid and there is so much data available, some useful and some not, that the answer to the challenge is one none of us wants to hear. It's just going to take some time. We need time to realign our processes and transition to our new way of thinking in healthcare.

> Fundamentally, every medical record is a tool for collecting information: the information a physician collects when looking at you in a physical examination; the results of lab tests. The constant automatic information collection is going to increase, whether it's your phone monitoring your heart rate or your scale sending information about your weight to your health provider, or the contact lenses Google wants to market that measure blood glucose levels.
>
> They all are sources of information about your health and well-being. And the challenge we face collectively, inside the health-care establishment and outside it, is how to take all this information, separate what's useful from what's not, and then apply it to improve the decisions of patients and care providers.

—David Blumenthal (Quoted in Fallows, 2014)

Everyone in healthcare is adapting, from the patients and physicians in a clinic office to the back-end staff and administrators trying to understand the right amount of investment and value that's embedded in this data. What we all want is to strike the right balance; we want to use and manage data, not become a slave to it. The future and the potential of data hints that if we can find that right balance, our organizations and the care that they provide will become more effective, safer, and better aligned with cost. That is the goal of any data-driven healthcare organization.

THE GAP

For years, my family had no idea what I did for a living. For a while, they wondered if the job I claimed to have was just a confusing cover-up for a covert lifestyle, perhaps with the CIA. Now when I tell people what I do, the response is always "You must be really busy." Is it possible that in 15 years it went from being so elusive it made more sense that I was a spy, to so common the middle-aged woman, seated next to me on a flight, knew exactly what I was talking about?

> *There are no easy answers; you better understand your data.*
>
> —Jeff Burke, Executive Advisor, Bon Secours Health System

I'm finally part of the in crowd. My early collegial connection to analysis seemed to seal my fate as a data wonk. Then, lo and behold, the *Harvard Business Review* said in 2012 that the data scientist is the sexiest job of the twenty-first century (Davenport and Patil, 2012). Finally, my patience paid off. But what does that really mean? What does it mean to be a data scientist? What does it mean to be data driven? What does it mean to invest in data? Not that many years ago, I had to work really hard to prove to healthcare organizations that data was the way forward. Today, I find myself trying to be heard above the noise. Data has become so ubiquitous, so popularized that we've forgotten what it really takes to do the work. We've fallen victim to the "Keeping Up with the Joneses: Data Edition." We can't articulate the value that data will provide for our own organization. In our fast-paced, soda-pop, YouTube-clip world, data has become a Hollywood starlet. We put you on a pedestal and then beat it down. We need you, we want you, yet we don't want to invest in you.

If I sound frustrated, it's because I am. At least once a month I get a call from the executive of a healthcare company that goes something like this:

"Laura, we've spent a year and a million dollars and we don't have anything to show for it."

"What was your goal?"

"To do BI."

"Okay, what do you have now?"

"A system that takes eight minutes to return one report that tells us how many patients we have."

I wish this was the exception. I'm still surprised that, for all the talk, when I get onsite at a hospital or health plan and start peeling back the layers I'm confronted with the reality that is healthcare—a data warehouse pulled together by transactional data experts at best, or at worst, a series of tables that were created by some savvy business users that's called a warehouse. The gap in the reality of what exists and the stuff you hear advertised in case studies is so large you can't see the other side.

DATA IS A FOUR-LETTER WORD

I still believe data is the way forward, but it's not an easy way forward. Creating a *data-driven healthcare organization (DDHO)* means that we have to slow down long enough to plan. We have to know and articulate the value that our data can bring to our organizations. But we also have to know when to say stop so we can reassess and reengage. Data can be powerful and valuable, but before it becomes that, it can be an unforgiving master. We have to change the culture of healthcare to become a data-driven industry. We have to get rid of the naysayers and stop thinking about data as either our salvation or our end. It's just data. It's neither good nor bad. It's what you do with it that matters.

First, let's determine if becoming data driven is the right thing for the industry or, more specifically, your organization. During my corporate life I've had to write a number of SWOT analyses. Popularized as a matrix, it breaks down the *strengths, weaknesses, opportunities,* and *threats* of a project or program (Wikipedia Contributors, 2013). (See Figure 1.1.)

	Helpful	Harmful
Internal — S	Powerful case studies from power users Current value of key report Knowledge of data and organization	W — Data silos Lack of focus Perception of value versus cost Previous failed attempts
External — O	Competitors are doing it Expectation from customers/stakeholders Entire cottage industry Legislation (HITECH and ACA) Technology advances	T — Confusing, conflicting advice Focus on hot topics distracts from the work Lack of standardization

Figure 1.1 SWOT

This SWOT analysis for becoming a data-driven healthcare organization is generic, but I encourage you to take this framework and fill it in for yourself to see if becoming a DDHO makes sense for you. We want to find a way to leverage the strengths and exploit the opportunities while managing the weaknesses and reducing the threats.

Strengths

In this case, we have to find a way to take those individual case studies where a power user found value in data and expand that to other departments or advance the skill set to other individuals. In addition, we can take some of the key reports, the ones that are used the most frequently, and try to improve on them or send them to a broader (appropriate) audience. We need to account for the way in which our organization works; whether it is decision by committee or a strong hierarchal chain of command, having internal resources who know and understand how things get done is critical to taking the program to the next level. Finally, we can take advantage of our internal depth of knowledge of our own data, which is invaluable as we begin this journey. That collective knowledge in your organization needs to be empowered to be brought together and incentivized to work together to break down any barriers, perceived or real, that impede the organization's ability to utilize its own integrated data.

Weaknesses

Internally, we have data silos that have these organizational moats around them. These aren't grain silos; they're missile silos (as my friend Skip said to me a few years ago). Regardless, the value of that data isn't realized until the data is out of the silos and integrated with other data. So breaking down the silos has to be done.

Organizationally, I find that the lack of focus or a strategic plan around data impedes a lot of progress. In order to manage data like an asset, we have to think of it like an asset. We also have to work around the perception of value versus cost. The value and understanding of what the data can bring to the entire organization has to be well communicated and well understood; otherwise, you risk having naysayers slow down the progress of the effort. This can also happen if you've had past failed attempts. We've all been there; no project is perfect. The best thing you can do is learn from past mistakes and move on.

Very large organizations will struggle with this, just by the nature of being large. Communicating out to a big, dispersed organization in a manner that is effective and timely is a challenge in and of itself.

Opportunities

The year of healthcare data is here; 2014 has seen some of the most significant changes in data in memory. That is represented by the number of opportunities that were identified. First and foremost, both the Affordable Care Act (ACA) and the HITECH Act ushered in the era of data for healthcare. Once that happened, an entire industry was created practically overnight that addresses data in healthcare (see the next section, "Threats"). The quantified self-movement and the concomitant "wearables" prompted an increased expectation by all customers for better and more frequent data. Your members, patients, providers, and brokers all want visually impactful and timely dashboards. Finally, there's the whole "Everyone else is doing it." It's true that many other healthcare organizations have started down this path. Some have led boldly, adopting enterprise data warehouses early in their maturity, but most jumped on the bandwagon post the passing of the HITECH Act in 2009. All these opportunities mean that if your competitors are doing it, your customers are asking for it, and entrepreneurs are creating for it, there is something very powerful there.

Threats

If you follow my content at all, books, webinars, articles, and so on, you know that I'm a pessimist. The threats section in most of my SWOT analyses tends to be a vent box that resembles my level of frustration.

It's true; an entire cottage industry and associated experts were newly minted the day after the HITECH Act was signed. What have evolved from that are some products and services that are nothing more than words on glossy brochures; in some cases they provide flat-out wrong advice. The challenge that healthcare has is that we are a relatively immature technology-purchasing audience. No doubt we can buy the best of the MRI machines out there. But the subtleties of purchasing software or investing in very specific healthcare BI services associated with data that is relatively new to the organization can thwart the most careful organizations. Therefore, the biggest threat I see to our ability to become a true DDHO is the same thing that's an opportunity: the industry itself. Organizations that have hired chief information officers from other industries or asked a consultant to help in purchase cycles might be the best way to mitigate this formidable risk.

Energy and persistence conquer all things.

—Benjamin Franklin

SETTING THE STAGE

Amid the chaos, a question: Is it worth it to you and your organization to become data driven? If the answer is yes, then this book is for you. In this book, I map out the major efforts associated with becoming a data-driven healthcare organization.

First, we have to understand what happens when we use data to transform an industry. In Chapter 2, I outline the value of data and what it takes to make changes on such a massive scale. In addition, I introduce the RISE methodology. This framework allows us to quickly fill the innovation gap that exists for healthcare while managing the risk as best as possible.

Chapter 3 addresses a significant issue facing data in healthcare today, standardization—or perhaps more appropriately, *lack* of standardization. Interviews and research show the impact of standards in healthcare, and do present a significant issue when comparing organizations to one another. No book on data-driven healthcare would be complete without a fair assessment of the impact of standards.

In Chapter 4, we take a deep-dive into technology, or as deep as this business-minded, self-proclaimed "not-a-technologist" is willing to go. I went pretty far. What I learned in writing these first few chapters is that much of the success of data-driven healthcare lies in our ability to close the innovation gap by using cutting-edge technology. After months of formal and informal conversations and research into alternative methodologies for moving and storing data, this chapter was born. I believe it presents our best options for adapting quickly to our brave new world.

Of course, in order to become a DDHO, we have to address the cultural impact of such a change. Chapter 5 outlines what it will take for your organization to make the shift. This isn't a quick-fix effort. It will take months, perhaps even years, before your organization can claim success. But in this chapter I outline the three things that your organization can do, from training, to marketing, to more traditional departments like information technology and informatics, to make sure everyone, from the executive assistants to the CEO, is data driven.

Chapter 6 attempts to make sense of the booming industry of big data. The term is so ubiquitous that I have even heard it on the evening news, yet we know little about what it is and how it can help solve the real and complicated problems of healthcare. This chapter reviews a few organizations that have dipped their toe in the big data lake. We can learn from their stories to see how big data can help us on the DDHO journey.

The most exciting chapter in the book is Chapter 7. The future of *healthcare business intelligence (BI)* is with the patient. I made that statement in *Healthcare Business Intelligence.* That's a shift that is started, with apps that allow you to measure movement and sleep. Eventually we will connect all of these data with our personal health record (PHR) and have a more robust version of what individual patients actually do (versus what they say they do) to take care of their health. The powerful individual case studies of personalized medicine and the quantified-self movement will shift over time toward healthcare delivery, and we will have to find a way to present that. The closer we get to this, the more data will become a part of the solution instead of a part of the problem.

Using average healthcare consumers as a test bed, and relying on some graphic artists for creative support, I've outlined six best practices for visualizing data to patients and members. This audience has different expectations than our internal audience or even our customers (brokers and providers, e.g.). If you're not visualizing data to patients now, you will be soon. These best practices will be important to adopt to ensure that we give our patients and members the best information to make important decisions.

Chapter 8 gets about as provocative as this subject can get. Because we know that our audience is shifting from an internal one to an external one, we have to address privacy and confidentiality. This is an incredibly dynamic subject. During discussions with average healthcare consumers (my version of "on the street"), there is a distinct gap in what 20-somethings feel is appropriate privacy and confidentiality compared to what my generation and older feel is appropriate. Protecting data is still an important part of the work, and we will discuss the processes that can ensure that your organization is protected as you enter your DDHO journey.

Finally, Chapter 9 outlines what you have to do in the next year to take the first steps in your DDHO journey. My hope is that this very pragmatic approach leaves you with a tangible set of steps that you can use as soon as you close the book.

IS THIS BOOK FOR YOU?

If you're still not sure if this book is for you, let me offer this. If you firmly believe, as I do, that most healthcare companies can get more value out of data than they do today, this book is for you. If you believe, like I do, that most healthcare organizations aren't really sure what the next step is so they don't take one, this book is for you. If you believe, as I do, that if we could just "up our game," healthcare would improve, this book is for you. Even if you're just curious as to what it would take, this book is for you. Read it in good health.

REFERENCES

Davenport, T. H., and D. J. Patil. (2012, October). "Data Scientist: The Sexiest Job of the 21st Century." *Harvard Business Review*. Retrieved October 22, 2013, from http://hbr.org/2012/10/data-scientist-the-sexiest-job-of-the-21st-century/.

Fallows, J. (2014, March 19). "Why Doctors Still Use Pen and Paper." *The Atlantic*. Retrieved March 26, 2014, from http://www.theatlantic.com/magazine/archive/2014/04/the-paper-cure/358639/.

Merriam-Webster. (2014). Definition, "Data." Retrieved March 26, 2014, from *Merriam-Webster Dictionary*: http://www.merriam-webster.com/dictionary/data.

Wikipedia Contributors. (2013, October 22). *Wikipedia*. Retrieved October 22, 2013, from http://en.wikipedia.org/wiki/SWOT_analysis.

CHAPTER 2

What Happens When You Use Data to Transform an Industry?

The questions we ask change the thing we make.

—Seth Godin

I haven't been feeling well lately. I've been more tired than usual; I've experienced some dizzy spells and other odd, seemingly unrelated symptoms—eye-twitching, ear-ringing, sudden weight changes, and difficulty sleeping. As the symptoms seem to mount I call my care coordinator, a person who represents both the insurance company and my provider. They review my history, including the recent addition of my DNA profile that I've received through an independent organization. Based on my genetic risk factors of age, gender, and so on, she recommends that I see an endocrinologist. An appointment is scheduled right then, and a few days later I walk into the clinic and check in. I don't have to fill out any additional paperwork; they know who I am, why I'm there, my birth date, and all other relevant information.

The initial clinical assessment includes checking my weight and blood pressure. The nurse asks if anything has changed since the phone call and confirms any new medications since the last recording. I report nothing new and within a few moments the nurse sends me to lab for a blood draw. After a short wait the doctor comes in and sits across from me to have a discussion. She holds a tablet in her hand; there is no computer screen anywhere in the room and she makes no attempt to distract herself from our conversation about my health, she just asks me about my symptoms, their frequency, and the level to which they disrupt my daily life. As we talk the lab results return, on her tablet, with a subtle pop-up box. They confirm what the data supported; my thyroid seems to be out of balance.

The next few months are a progression toward management of my thyroid. A physical exam showed no sign of a tumor, so no advanced imaging test was ordered, saving me some stress and my insurance company some money. Additional care providers were added to my team, including an acupuncturist, who helps me with some of the symptoms and stress management, which seems to have exacerbated my symptoms. I know this because I kept an application (app), a symptom tracker, on my iPhone that sent data to my doctor. It was just one app of a couple that were used to track my medication adherence, important when managing my thyroid and trying to find the right pharmaceutical mix; it tracked my food intake, activity, and stress level, sending all of the information wirelessly back to my electronic health records (EHRs), where my care coordination team, the one I originally called, could track that data and in cooperation with my physician determine the next best steps in my care—all without stepping foot into a clinic.

An additional app helps me keep track of the expenses, including bills for the care I received and the balance of my health savings account (HSA). It even allows me to pay the bill or send questions to the claims department. I didn't even have to call to get preapproval for my acupuncturist, because she was part of the care team.

You may be asking yourself right now, where is this wonderful place and how can I go there? Well, this isn't a real place; it's my version of the future of healthcare, upheld by the data points that are now available and pervasive. It outlines the integration of our providers and payers together—the *care coordination* team that is a result of the accountable care organizations and patient-centered medical home. It's aligned by the data, from DNA profiles, EHRs, clinical trials, financials, and "wearables" that provide the level of activity, heart rate, and blood pressure to my smart phone applications. All of these data are brought together to deliver good, quality care in a manner in which most patients want to experience it. We are not so far away from this new reality; it is just beyond the horizon, but between us and this new reality is an abyss.

THE HISTORY OF CHANGE

I originally became very excited about writing this book in August 2012, the month my first book was published. I had been doing some research for a keynote I was delivering and started thinking about how data has already changed healthcare in many ways over the years.

It came to me as a result of learning of the evolution of the American Cancer Society, the time before clinical trials were what we know them to be today. In 1962, the five-year survival rate for non-Hodgkin's lymphoma was just 7 percent; it was also the year my dad was diagnosed with non-Hodgkin's lymphoma. Just four years prior happened to be a pivotal year for cancer research, when the American Cancer Society was restructured and data from many different experiments (hardly the rigor we know of today with clinical trials) was brought together to help cure some of the most devastating of cancers (Mukherjee, 2010). The cancer that drove most cancer researchers at the time, because it was almost always diagnosed in the very young, was acute lymphoblastic leukemia (ALL). In 1962, it had just a 5 percent five-year survival rate. Today, there is a 94 percent five-year survival rate. In 2006, my nephew was diagnosed with ALL. In 2008, my sister was diagnosed with breast cancer. (See Figure 2.1.)

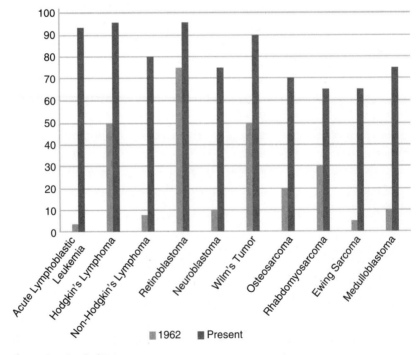

Figure 2.1 Survival Rate

A cure for cancer has been elusive. Decades of research and billions of dollars later, we have changed the reality for cancer survivors. Of course, it's not perfect, but it's much better, and much of it was due to some simple steps:

1. Focused attention on an issue
2. Data brought together from disparate sources
3. A new way of thinking and talking about cancer

What happens when you think about a problem in a new way? What happens when collaboration is something that is encouraged rather than avoided? What happens when you ask questions that seem impossible to achieve? Ask my dad, a 50-year survivor of a cancer that killed 96 percent of its victims. Ask my nephew, a healthy nine-year-old with a quick smile and a level of gratitude you usually see in adults, or ask my sister, who blessedly celebrates her five-year mark from remission in just a few months. Better care is what happens when you become data driven. Thriving is what happens when you become data driven.

ON THE BRINK

Change is happening today with the advent of *big data*, including the ability to map your personal DNA for $99 and the massive amounts of clinical data from EHRs. We are changing healthcare every day. Yet so much of it is staying the same. So much of it is frustratingly slow and behind the adoption curve. But changing healthcare in this way, to become truly data driven, is radical—so radical that it may just work.

In the course of working on this book, I have really struggled with the abyss. The reality of what exists in most healthcare organizations, the ones that I see every day, is so far behind what is ideal from a business intelligence and data management perspective that even thinking about being data driven seems hopeful at best and cruel at worst.

The abyss is prolific. It exists in every aspect of data management in healthcare and much of that work remains in the operational and administrative part of our organizations. But some of the most difficult work is finding a way to bridge the gap in the leadership and management of our hospitals. We have to start talking and thinking about using data in a different way. Data management doesn't occur in a data warehouse somewhere; it occurs in the management layers of our organizations.

The only way that we can fix the gap is if we acknowledge the reality of what exists today for the vast majority of hospitals and healthcare organizations. We are not in a position to really use the data that we have. Forget about big data; we can't even effectively manage and use the "regular" data. That data has everything we need to make my story a reality, yet we still can't use it because there are so many barriers. It's not accessible, it's not collected in a way that allows us to compare, it's not timely, it represents merely a sample of the population, we're afraid that it isn't right, or we're afraid that it is right.

WHAT IS "DATA DRIVEN," AND WHY DOES IT MATTER?

I was a data geek before being a data geek was cool. I have always quantified decisions. My life, both business and personal, is run on an Excel sheet. When I got married, my future in-laws stood slack-jawed as I showed them my massive Excel sheet that had every detail about my wedding. So, when the quantified self-movement started I knew that I would end up participating, first, through "23 and Me" (https://www.23andme.com/), a personal DNA analysis organization. I was thrilled with the idea that, for a small fee, I could have my DNA analyzed. Then, in May, I was waiting for my flight in San Francisco when I glanced over and the tagline "wouldn't you like a way to check in with yourself" caught my eye. "Up" by Jawbone is one of the many products that are available today to track your movement, sleep, and food intake. You plug it into a smart phone to get the data to download and be visualized to show your movement and sleep against a goal. At first, my behavior didn't change. But then I started to see the trend over time and realized that thanks to my job of sitting at a computer or flying around, I sit too much. This awareness prompted me to sign up for a 5K run. Thanks to the contextual, visual data, I modified my behavior. On a larger scale, this is the change that we have to propagate for our organizations.

The only reason we have invested and adopted *BI* (*business intelligence*) programs is because we want to be data driven. We want our organizations to transition from decision-making-by-instinct to decision-making-by-data. We want this because we know that it can help deliver better, faster, and more appropriate care to our friends and family— our patients.

First, let's define what it means to be data driven. In order for your organization to really take advantage of the data, it must be consumable and contextual, to encourage action that will modify behaviors over time.

Data driven means that information must be consumable and contextual, to encourage action that will modify behavior over time.

One of the most important factors of a data-driven organization is a broad adoption by all kinds of different users, inside and outside your organization. That requires a new set of thinking on how data is presented. Some users will be clinicians and some will not. One of the key factors of a data-driven healthcare organization (DDHO) is that the information that is provided changes behavior over time, but that cannot happen if the information is delivered only to a subset of users or via a siloed data set.

It is important to note that to be data driven does not mean to be a slave to data. This will pose a management and a regulatory challenge. Becoming a slave to data, something that can happen if you acquiesce to the pressure of big data and other trends, spells disaster for any organization that is looking to change its behavior based on what it learns from data. Big data is tempting, and can be revolutionary, but more isn't always better and big data is far from a silver bullet. You cannot learn from data if you simply go through the motions to ensure that you were able to check the box. You can't really learn much from *data* at all. What you can learn from is *information*, the type of information that is timely, contextual, and relevant. So much of what a healthcare organization produces today is none of those things. Even *meaningful use*, which is an incredible stride in the right direction, doesn't really provide meaningful information if you don't look for it, and so many healthcare organization don't have the time to look for it.

MANAGEMENT AND MEASUREMENT

There is a famous quote, "You can't manage what you don't measure" (W. Edwards Deming). If you're a healthcare administrator or CEO, I'd like to ask you a question: What *don't* you measure? A few years ago I was talking with a friend of mine, and he said that his hospital had to produce over 1,500 regulatory reports a year. With all of that regulatory reporting, on a variety of different data elements and in most cases less-than-useful data, what in the world are we measuring, changing, or achieving?

Healthcare measures everything but uses too little of that data to actually modify processes or improve methods (and therefore outcomes). Too much measurement means that there is no opportunity for action, and that is where change happens. Our data warehouses have paid the price. With little time to stop and think about what we are building, we have simply thrown data together, used Excel worksheets as a source of data, and relied heavily on smart analysts to hold our organizations together.

The end result of this is the fiefdoms around the data. Analysts who have created all of our reports hold the organizational lexicon in their heads, and losing one analyst means a big impact to your organization; or just as bad, they hold that data as close to the vest as possible, not sharing or integrating with other data points. That is not a scalable or flexible option.

Today, we have healthcare organizations that are ready to change, know they need to change, recognize the value of data, but don't know where to start. A revolution has to occur—not a small, slow change but a drastic and dynamic leap over the abyss.

Deming, the man most often credited with the quote "You can't manage what you don't measure," was a famous statistician and one whose work bears an incredible amount of relevance for today's data-intensive

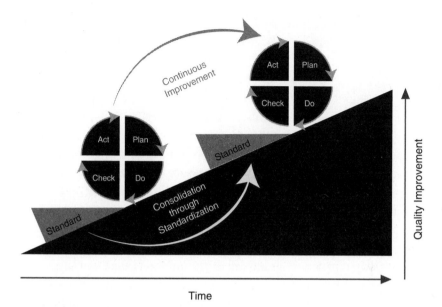

Figure 2.2 PDCA Cycle
Source: Johannes Vietze.

healthcare organization. His method, "Plan, Do, Check, Act," provides a model for the work that we will need to undertake if we want to become DDHOs. (See Figure 2.2.)

This cycle got me to thinking. What is the best way to spur innovation while managing risk? It's critical for healthcare organizations to move faster, but we don't have time to make a lot of the mistakes that can occur because of this accelerated timeline.

PLANNING THE APPROACH

Every year there are business metaphors that get overused and underappreciated. One I hear very often is the "30,000-foot view," sometimes that of the data, as in getting a high-level understanding of what the data is indicating and sometimes it's about the project itself. Then, if it's a really good analogy, it's followed up with "We need to make sure we have plenty of runway." This got me to thinking, as I sit here in this airplane, what does it mean to be at 30,000 feet? What is just enough runway?

A number of factors influence a successful landing. Some of them are flexible, others are not. Let's consider briefly the factors: the aircraft, the crew, the weather, the weight of the aircraft, and the destination. We can manipulate all of those factors to some degree, but once you're in flight, you cannot change the crew or the aircraft. You can fly around weather, but that will change your destination (potentially), and you can drop weight if absolutely necessary but only in the form of fuel, which of course has other serious ramifications. Eventually the aircraft has to land, and the speed, distance, and altitude are the key performance indicators that can be aligned to best practices. What you will notice is that depending on where you are in your journey, your key performance indicators change. It could be said, in air travel and in data warehousing, that any landing you walk away from is a good one.

For our purposes, the aircraft is the products that you use, both back-end systems and front-end BI products. The crew is represented by your project staff. The weight of the aircraft is represented by your data; the weather is your broader organization and external influences like the federal government. Finally, the destination is the vision you have for data in your organization. My point to this rather elaborate analogy is that if you can *reduce the unknowns, identify alternatives, streamline the standards,* and *evaluate the activities* (RISE), you can close the gap on these activities and improve the innovation cycle in your organization.

RISE

Creating a methodology that's specific to healthcare's adaption to data may seem daunting. It wasn't the initial goal of this book. But the more research I did and the more conversations I had, the more I realized that there isn't a good framework for this work. Sure, there are maturity cycles and development cycles, but there isn't a framework that helps us iterate through each of those cycles successfully. In other words, we had no way of repeatedly performing the work with enough consistency to ensure results. The RISE methodology allows us to do that, by focusing on the things that impede rapid innovation in healthcare. (See Figure 2.3.)

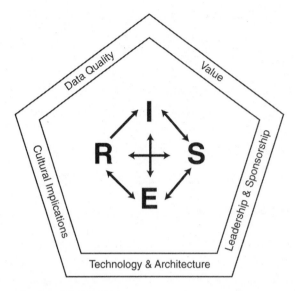

Figure 2.3 RISE Model

Reduce the Unknowns

One of the most significant issues facing healthcare today is the disparate data. Frankly, it's all over the board. Of course, standards are an issue, but even without the constraints of standards, most hospitals and healthcare organizations have such a broad variety of data and ranging quality of the data that just getting a standard file format out the door seems like a monumental effort. Much of the daily work that I do is talking with healthcare organizations about how they can manage this disparate, random, and challenging asset. Forcing standardization isn't an option, so what we have to do is remove the unknowns.

When I was working on my master's degree, I wrote a thesis researching the causal effect between depression and chronic pain. I used a little-known regression test called "Two-Stage Least Squares." In lay terms, I was looking to control for intervening variables to determine if there was one factor that was more statistically responsible for the causation. I spent hours in the computer lab running test after test. The intent of the effort was to remove the unknowns. In the first step of the RISE model we have to do the same thing, but that requires us to discuss the problem in a way that we likely haven't discussed it before. When I was working on my thesis, I had the advantage of the data mining to tell me what variables consistently intervened. In most cases you won't have that data, but what you will have is the knowledge of your organization and previous attempts at similar efforts. You can discuss these and document them as much as possible, yet know that the whole point of RISE and specifically reducing the unknowns is that you have to revisit it over time. As our programs move along, our variables change.

Identify the Alternatives

Closing the gap won't be easy. The traditional method of data warehousing is probably too slow; we have to accelerate ahead of many other industries in an attempt to save ourselves. That means that we have to become very good at identifying alternatives quickly, and fail early and often. We may find that a pilot program associated with big data doesn't work the way we thought but it points out another alternative that we hadn't considered before. Despite the name, we don't just want to identify the alternatives; we actually want to test to see if they work. Don't do it on the full scale, but smaller pilots and proofs of concepts will allow us to iterate quickly through new processes and products to determine which ones will be the most beneficial to close the innovation gap.

Streamline the Standards

The focus of this part of the methodology is to ensure that standards are identified and adopted into the integrated data warehouse. This is important because that is where your average business user will access the data and reports associated with your organization. The standards, therefore, must be part of the standard governance process and adapted by the organization in alignment with the industry. There are so many standards that can be applied; it's important to recognize that the assessment of standards is an effort in and of itself. The governance group is the most logical place for this to happen, but just like the rest of the RISE model, it must do so in an iterative and timely manner. These standards could also impact the alternatives that you work to identify. Since there may be a number of standards that you can adopt, identifying the key standards and running a pilot or proof of concept as part of the alternative analysis is prudent.

Evaluate the Activities

This final step in the model is the key to its success. The iterative, agile nature of RISE requires the adapter to be willing and able to evaluate all aspects of the program and make adjustments as needed to ensure success. Every aspect of the program is up for debate, discussion, and adjustment. The most effective way to ensure that you are able to do this is to create, as you begin, a set of success criteria that you will use to evaluate all aspects of the program to ensure that everything you do is aligned to delivering value, quality, and success. Anything else should be reconsidered or removed.

CHANGE MECHANISMS OF RISE

The RISE model creates a framework in which you can begin the work of becoming data driven. First, it's important to review some of the factors that I see that often undermine these types of efforts.

1. *Stop all the insanity.* That's the politics around who owns the data. We are all stewards of this data; none of us *owns* it. That perspective kills the rapid innovation that has to occur.

2. *Strip it to the basics.* We're talking about patients and the care they receive, by whom, and when/where. Those are the key factors that we are looking at. Sometimes we care about the financial aspect of that, and that's okay, but as long as we know the *who, when, where,* and (sometimes) *how,* getting to the *how much* should be pretty easy.

3. *Demand control of the data.* This is a holdover from my last book, *Healthcare Business Intelligence* (Wiley, 2012) but the fact is we are not in control of most of the sources of this information; yet

without integrating the data, it's really tough for me to tell you what our patients did, when, and where (our basics), so we have to get our data out of the black boxes that are the point solutions of vendors. We need their systems and their transactional expertise, but we don't need or want them to tell us how to integrate and use the data.

4. *Integrate and repeat.* Stop overthinking the data. Let's work hard to get it in a spot where we can start *using* it. That doesn't mean that we skip all of the data-quality work that we know is important, but let's not boil the ocean. Pick some facts and attributes (remember our basics) and go from there. Schedule sprints and integrate just two or three data points in a few weeks, rinse, and repeat.

5. *Make it consumable.* We have to provide a visual medium as access to this data. That requires some planning, particularly if you don't have a product that supports that effort. Remember that it has to be contextual in order to increase your user base.

6. *Get it out there.* As fast as you can create it, get it out there for others to use. We're looking to feed the innovation engine, not to release the perfect thing.

RISE	Reduce the Unknowns	Identify Alternatives	Streamline Standards	Evaluate the Program
What	Understand the program (or the problem) as thoroughly as possible.	Identify the alternatives that can help manage the unknowns.	Adapt standards through governance process prior to implementation.	Make modifications to processes and objectives to improve results.
How	During an initial kickoff session with key stakeholders, discuss the program from all facets and highlight risks or areas of unknowns that present risk.	From the list of risks or unknowns, identify the alternatives that can help control the risks. Plan on short, iterative pilots to test out impact.	Constant review of industry standards should be part of a governance program. When a new standard is proposed, analyze for impact and then review and approve through governance prior to implementation.	Immediately following the initial kickoff, create the program's success factors, criteria that will allow you to determine the effectiveness of any aspect of the program.

REVOLUTION

This radical shift has to start today. No revolution ever occurred by taking slow and deliberate steps. Besides, that option has already been decided for us, as much of the change happening in healthcare today was precipitated by political powers that be. The change is already happening. We are teetering on the brink, and if you don't start to steer, you can't control the dive. The changes that are just beyond our reach will become tomorrow's reality. It's up to us to see our organizations through the free fall. We can do that by adapting the change mechanisms, applying the RISE methodology, and adopting the mantra that *done* is better than perfect.

REFERENCES

23 and Me. (n.d.). 23 and Me. Retrieved from https://www.23andme.com/.
Mukherjee, S. (2010). *The Emperor of all Maladies: A Biography of Cancer*. New York: Scribner.

CHAPTER **3**

How the Lack of Data Standardization Impedes Data-Driven Healthcare

anaging disparate data is what we do as data warehouse professionals. Integrating data together to get a full picture of entities like patients, physicians, procedures, financials, and facilities (and so on) is the bread and butter of data warehousing, and it's the heart of what makes data warehouses so useful.

For many years, really until 2009, a data warehouse in a healthcare organization was not the norm. Many of the big guys did it, including UnitedHealth Group, UPMC, and Mayo, but for the rest of the payers and providers out there, the return on investment wasn't certain enough to risk the investment. I don't think most healthcare organizations came to data warehousing subsequent to 2009 knowingly. They were too focused on meeting meaningful-use criteria. Then stage-two requirements came along, and it became obvious that maintaining a population so that you can compare their outcomes over time was not the sweet spot of most transactional-based electronic health records (EHRs). Enter the *data warehouse*.

This accelerated adoption spawned innovation and creative methods of addressing the long-standing and challenging issues in healthcare from outside the industry. Yet we still struggle with basic activities and using data warehouse best practices for healthcare. First and foremost, in order to become a data-driven healthcare organization (DDHO), we need data. But not just any data, and the data can't just be in any form. The entire focus on becoming data driven is to provide data to everyone in the organization to improve decision making. We have to learn from other industries and their approaches to providing data and analytics to business users.

HEALTHCARE DATA COMPLEXITY

Applying well-adopted standards to healthcare just makes good sense. Many healthcare organizations have discussed the need for us to look outside of the industry for innovation and leadership, and data warehousing is no different. We can learn a lot from those industries that have been doing data warehousing for a long time.

Complexity is something I hear a lot in healthcare; while other industries may be complex, the degree to that complexity is on a lower scale.

As I mentioned in *Healthcare Business Intelligence* (Madsen, 2012), I spoke with some of the leading data architects in the industry who wouldn't touch healthcare data because it was so messy. That continues to be true, and the impact of investing in the wrong resources continues to be significant. A few months ago I spoke with a professional healthcare association that had spent two years and over a million dollars, and their chief financial officer admitted to me that they had very little to show for it. The one thing that really gets me upset over the current state of healthcare business intelligence is that the failure rate of data warehouses is unreasonably high because we insist on making mistakes that are costly, unnecessary, and often motivated by political positioning rather than what is truly good for the organization and the industry as a whole. It's not so complicated that we can't solve for it.

Moving Data

First, we have to move data out of our transactional systems. Transactional systems are any systems that we use in the course of transacting the business of healthcare. That includes electronic health records (EHRs), financial systems, workforce systems, customer relationship management (CRM), or enterprise resource planning (ERP). In this first step there are a surprising number of subtleties that are specific to healthcare. You have to get the data out of those transactional systems to buffer the data from the performance degradation of queries. In addition, taking data items out of their source systems provides the opportunity to apply transformations or modifications that ensure that the data is usable.

The important thing here is that you don't try to make this step too complicated. Best practice still recommends that a staging area is sufficient for most uses. Many healthcare organizations I see try to create *mirrored databases*. It sounds like the easiest thing to do at the time, but long-term maintenance means another step in your process to ensure that the data really is mirrored. I can't tell you how many times I've worked on projects that had so-called mirrored databases only to find out the mirror has its own rules in it, making regression testing very challenging.

Procedurally, taking data out is much more complicated because of the systems we work with. Depending on your particular situation, you may be at the mercy of proprietary data warehouses that are "features" of your EHR implementation, for example. Some of these systems are very well done, and others not so much. One of the advantages to integrating your data in your DW is the control you have over that data. You don't have to wait around for someone to make the changes that you need, and you certainly are not reliant on resources that a couple hundred other customers are relying on. These systems are often black boxes, and you may find yourself with very limited transparency to the data and the rules that are applied.

You may find yourself in this situation through no fault of your own. If that's the case, try working with the vendor in question to determine if data feeds are a possibility (for those that don't provide you access to a data warehouse). There's often an additional fee or changes to the contract language. You have to be careful about changes in those data feeds. The vendor should warn you with plenty of time to make modifications when they're going to make a change that will materially impact the data. Obviously, lots of data feeds aren't optimal, and thankfully they are becoming less the norm than just three years ago. However, the "data warehouses" that come along for the ride with the EHRs aren't really all they're cracked up to be, and some of them are so complex with so much embedded logic that healthcare organizations are asking vendors to peel back the layers and send the base data. I sat with a director of business intelligence a year ago, and behind his desk was the data schematic from their EHR vendor. It was a plat printout that was easily four feet by four feet. As we talked, he pointed to it a couple of times, making his point about fuzzy logic and missed table joins. He complained about the vendor's product management advisory board, of which he was a member. His requested changes would take years to implement, he was told. He didn't have years to achieve the level of reporting that was required to compete in the market—he had months.

Data Is *Your* Asset—Manage It That Way

Control is still the name of the game in these instances. Let's be clear— a data warehouse dedicated to your EHR is great and will provide you a lot of value with embedded alerts and meaningful-use reporting, but it's not integrated with the rest of your systems and therefore presents merely part of the picture.

The data warehousing industry often refers to a *system of record*— the one system, or software, where the data (usually) originates and that serves as the one true point. Let's think about it like the North Star. In financial services, their system of record is what they often refer to as the *core system*. It's the transactional system that houses all of their activities. For our purposes, healthcare has multiple core systems. The EHR is one of them, but that doesn't include all of the information required to get a complete picture. So, we have to look to our practice management systems, workforce system or ERPs, the financial systems, and many other entities.

Once we get the data out, we have to place it somewhere. This phase is critically important in your pursuit of becoming a DDHO. Placing data in an appropriately structured data warehouse allows for scalability, reusability, flexibility, and all of those other important features that we ascribe to data warehouses. But this step isn't without risk, and many times I see healthcare organizations trying to take shortcuts to get to the endpoint as fast as possible. Just yesterday, as I was pacing the hallway in a client's office in California, I got a call about another client on the East Coast. They are itching to make rapid progress on their data warehouse. They are feeling the pressure of their *accountable care organization (ACO)* partnership and have significant and valid concerns that they don't have the right skills on their team to create a best-in-class data warehouse. Their assessment is that they need to buy a product.

It's true that since the Affordable Care Act was signed, many organizations have popped up trying to solve for the data issues that we have in healthcare. Some of those products are great, well thought out and beneficial. Others are vaporware with a fancy front-end. It takes some due diligence to get past the surface to determine which is which.

Here's the issue with just "buying a product." First, it doesn't save you any time or money. Usually these products require a specific skill set from consultants who work for the company. Your organization will also have to invest in the person or persons to provide requirements and with whom you will sit side by side so that you are prepared to support the program once it's in your hands—unless you want to have consultants sitting there in perpetuity. Then there's the little question about integrating the data from other products (either other EHRs or staffing, time sheets, CRM, etc). Odds are, whatever product you buy will either limit the ability to integrate data from other systems or will pick a couple systems that they've created partnerships with. Guess what you end up with? You will have another silo of data that still doesn't give you a full picture of your member or patient population. Perhaps you think, "I will just take data out of this system and integrate it with this other product I bought." But getting data out of many of these systems (EHR, ERP, CRM) proves challenging because the vendors have a proprietary data model that they are not likely to expose so you can take your own data out.

Not only do I see this scenario play out in individual organizations; if you step back, you can see the implications throughout the industry. In a recent *Harvard Business Review* blog, authors Thomas Redman and Ronald Nielsen framed the situation eloquently:

> *As a first step, many organizations have recognized the need for common data terminologies (e.g., LOINC, SNOMED, ICD-9, HL-7, etc.) and developed their own. Further the Office of the National Coordinator (ONC) has set benchmarks that ensure at least minimal connectivity. Within the domains where they are used consistently, such terminologies and benchmarks are fine.*
>
> *But across the industry, they contribute to what we and others call "towers of medical Babel." The "Babel" is exacerbated by the proliferation of vendors, each with their own proprietary approaches, leading to each tower becoming thicker, better fortified, and more isolated from others.*
>
> *Source:* http://blogs.hbr.org/cs/2013/02/computerization_in_health_care.html.

STANDARDS . . . BECAUSE EVERYONE ELSE HAS THEM

What this all comes down to—the need for a data warehouse, the buy-or-build discussion—is the proliferation of standards but no consistency. Everyone has a standard, and their standard is the one that's required for one type of accreditation. But that standard doesn't align to the other five or six (or 12) that you have adopted. Creating a DDHO with a data warehouse that your average end user can consume requires a broad understanding and adoption of key standards, not everything and the kitchen sink.

This has led us to a dire situation within our organizations and throughout the industry. Adopted standards have limited value because of these silos. Standards are valuable only when they are adopted, shared, consistent, and stable. Data standards exist in healthcare; organizations like Health Level Seven (HL7) have been around for decades. The trouble that healthcare has is that everyone has their own standard. It's not that we lack standards; what we lack is *broadly adopted standards*.

Have you ever watched a group of six-year-olds play? I do, because I have one. If you get a couple of them together, pretty soon pretend-play starts and someone has to beat the bad guy. Each of the kids has their own rules, and they make them up as they go along. By the end of the game they are playing a completely different game and arguing about which one of them is right. That's a little like what healthcare data standards are right now. How can we adopt standards when no one knows the rules to align to? These siloed approaches to standards and benchmarks don't promote high standards; they actually do the opposite.

 ## DATA STANDARDS

A *standard* defines a frame of reference that encourages confidence between interacting parties. It serves as an agreement between two interacting parties to the context of the transaction.

Source: http://www.knowledge-integrity.com/columns/dmr200401.htm.

The implications are so broad-reaching it's hard to underestimate the impact. Even with the adoption of EHRs we find ourselves still struggling with a consistent set of standard data because the implementation included customizing the system to reflect your organization and its processes. This applies not only to the standard code sets like SNOMED and LOINC, but just as importantly to the use of responses for scenarios such as adverse events. Where some hospitals use a "Yes/No" to identify if any adverse event took place, others use a Likert Scale response set such as "Unlikely," "Likely," "Probably," and so forth. This misalignment, some yes/no responses and some on a scale, limits the comparison of the data, because it's challenging to know how to compare a "yes" response to a "likely" or "probable" response. Now imagine this occurring thousands of times with an exponential number of different scenarios (Kush et al., 2008).

 HL7 Mission Statement

CONCEPT

HL7 provides standards for interoperability that improve care delivery, optimize workflow, reduce ambiguity and enhance knowledge transfer among all of our stakeholders, including healthcare providers, government agencies, the vendor community, fellow SDOs and patients. In all of our processes we exhibit timeliness, scientific rigor and technical expertise without compromising transparency, accountability, practicality, or our willingness to put the needs of our stakeholders first.

—HL7, 2012

If you are like me, you are very well aware of HL7. I don't know one healthcare organization that isn't a member in some way, shape, or form. I've taken for granted the incredible amount of work that this organization has completed since its inception in 1987 to ensure that standards exist in healthcare. I recently spoke with Donald Mon, board chair for HL7. I asked him what kept him up at night; he said, "Too many things to mention." I asked him, "What is the biggest gap in healthcare data standards?" He said, "We need standardization of the clinical concepts."

This topic is also addressed in the article that appeared in the *New England Journal of Medicine* in 2008 (Kush et al., 2008). The idea is that in every healthcare organization there is an exponential number of differences that can occur for everything from taking a blood pressure to documenting an adverse event and everything in between. The trouble lies not only in the lack of consistency in how we define these things but in how we document them so that the data can be used in the multitude of ways needed to change healthcare with data. There are too many variations of the data that limit its usage. Until we have a systematic, consistent, and agreed-upon way of looking at clinical concepts, the heart of the work we do, we will continue to struggle.

But the biggest elephant in the room of data standards is the unique patient ID. Originally included in the HIPAA legislation in the early 1990s, it was quickly pulled out as a result of a rapid and virulent response from privacy groups. Without the ability to identify a unique patient, we limit our ability to treat a patient. It's too easy for me to be identified as Laura Madsen, Laura Fletcher, Laura Fletcher Madsen, or Lara Mattson. This scenario plays out a hundred (or more) times a day as people seek second opinions or advice from specialists. Cross-pollination of information about a patient even sometimes within the same health system is challenging, much more than it should be in 2014. The impact of a lack of a unique patient ID isn't too difficult to anticipate. As noted, I have my maiden name and my married name. Legally, I am Laura Fletcher Madsen, but that's too much to type or write so I just go by Laura Madsen. Since I've been married, I've changed jobs once and moved once. Thankfully, one's date of birth does not change, but believe it or not, that can be and often is reported erroneously because we ask people and people don't always tell the truth. In most instances, my healthcare payer and healthcare providers will attempt to isolate "Laura Madsen" by my name, address, and date of birth. In each case they will assign a member or patient ID. But what if, as is the case, I've changed my name and moved? No computer could know that Laura Fletcher from Bloomington, MN, is Laura Madsen from Burnsville, MN. At a minimum it would throw the records into an exception report that a person needs to review and determine if I am who I say I am. In most cases there's not enough to back up the idea that I am indeed one and the same. Now imagine that repeated thousands of times all over the country.

More disturbing to me, in the case of a unique patient identifier (UPI), is the idea that critical medical information about me is hidden somewhere. In most cases it takes me as an individual to relay information about my base medical demographics. My allergies, diagnosis, and preferences are all documented and codified but obscured.

What if I needed medical attention while I was incapacitated? How could I possibly relay that information then? They would never know that a very common pain medication causes a severe allergic reaction. There's only one way for them to find that out—trial and error. In other words, give it to me and see what happens.

In an era when I can buy various products with a push of a button on my phone or easily use ATMs all over the world to access funds from my Minnesota-based account, how is it that we are impaired with healthcare data to such a degree that receiving medical care while incapacitated could cause more harm than good?

Privacy advocates are strong voices against a UPI. They've vilified it as a gateway for hackers interested in your medical information and an invitation for patients to not share sensitive information. They advocate for a patient or individual to own their own healthcare data. They propose that access be provided via broad statements such as "If I need medical attention, I allow the treating physician to access my medical records." It's less clear to me where this statement would exist, or what would happen if the patient needed care while incapacitated. More important, do patients really want to manage their own data? I would be an advocate of individuals managing their own data; I think it's an ideal scenario, but it does not negate the need for a consistent method to identify an individual. Just because you manage your own data, likely in a cloud, doesn't mean that it can't fall into the wrong hands.

PARETO'S PRINCIPLE

Just as I started writing this book, I took a summer vacation. As I was packing I included my summer reading list: *The Emperor of All Maladies: The Data Model Resource Book, Volume 2* (Scribner, 2011), *Predictive Analytics* (Wiley, 2013), and *The One Thing* (Bard Press, 2013). I decided to read *The One Thing* first, thinking that it was the lightest of all the reads (to be fair, it's competing against some pretty heady stuff). Then, in Chapter 4, I run across something that clicks for me, something that frames up the data standards issue that healthcare has: the *80/20 rule*.

Most of us have some kind of exposure to the 80/20 rule. It's the idea, as posited by Italian economist Vilfredo Pareto, that wealth was not evenly distributed; it was first outlined by Joseph M. Juran as "Pareto's Principle of unequal distribution." I quickly jotted down: "Does this apply to data standards?" Have we spent our time on the 80 percent only to get 20 percent of the results? During my interview with Donald Mon, I asked him what his perspective was on all the different standards that existed in healthcare data, from LOINC to SNOMED.

> There is a lack of understanding between LOINC and SNOMED; they are a vocabulary, nomenclatures or coding (such as ICD), classification (such as LOINC), they are *complementary*. The challenge has been every time that you adopt something like a coding or classification it takes a long time, it's a big effort for healthcare organizations to develop them and then get them adopted. We have some of these things in a mature state, but we don't have a systematic way for how these things are being adopted (i.e., SNOMED is scientific for problem list).

So, these classifications, coding systems, vocabulary sets take time to implement and adopt and get us only about 20 percent of the value for 80 percent of the work. I don't think anyone takes away the value of these systems; if nothing else, they ensure we are talking the same language 20 percent of the time. Applying the 80/20 rule, though, means that now is the time to look at addressing the tougher pieces ahead, such as standardizing the clinical response sets of adverse events, or even how to document blood pressure in an EHR to ensure that we get 80 percent of the value out of the work that is ahead of us.

THE GREAT WALL OF DATA

We have built massive walls within and between our organizations. Those walls are made from data that represents millions of patients, procedures, diagnosis, and dollars. These walls are filled with information that can change the way healthcare in our country is delivered and the outcomes it achieves. We are each standing on our side of the wall, yelling at each other in different languages.

This book can't solve the political and socioeconomic factors that impact healthcare. That's not my specialty. I do, however, specialize in helping healthcare organizations use their data for the betterment of themselves and ourselves. We have to find a way over these great walls of data, and we should start with our own organizations and by breaking down the walls.

First, we have to reduce the silos in which our data sets exist. That includes the EHR and financial accounting systems that hold our data hostage. Regardless of the system and its role in your organization, you must find a way to get data out of proprietary data models and into highly integrated patient-based data models.

Second, we must apply consistency and standards to this data. That means addressing the issues of identifying and defining clinical concepts so that we all collect and deliver data on blood pressure or adverse events the same way.

Finally, being a DDHO requires *taking action,* using the data to improve healthcare delivery, efficiency, payment, and the experience. I don't underestimate what these three steps entail. These steps represent a major change in healthcare; so the question is, where do we start and how can we finish?

REFERENCES

HL7. (2012). *Health Level Seven International/About.* Retrieved July 3, 2013, from Health Level Seven International: http://www.hl7.org/about/index.cfm.

Kush, R. D., et al. (2008). "Electronic Health Records, Medical Research and the Tower of Babel." *New England Journal of Medicine,* 1738–1740. http://www.cdisc.org/system/files/all/reference_material/application/pdf/nejm_041708.pdf.

Madsen, L. B. (2012). *Healthcare Business Intelligence: A Guide to Empowering Successful Data Reporting and Analytics.* Hoboken, NJ: John Wiley & Sons.

CHAPTER 4

Adopting Your Data Warehouse for the Next Step in BI Maturity

get a lot of questions about data in the healthcare world. Some of the questions come from my dad on our weekly Sunday-morning phone calls, some of them from news outlets that interview me, and some from the people who hire me. Most of the questions revolve around one specific one: "How is it possible that we still don't know basic information about our patients, and their costs, and how can we fill the gap as fast as the industry needs us to?" The question is captivating. Healthcare has never been through this type of transformation in such a short amount of time.

As captivating as the question is, it's not easy to answer. I've thought about it a lot, I've lost sleep over it, and I've asked my friends and peers. The hard truth is we have to catapult our overburdened industry much farther than where we are today. The truth is that most of the organizations I work with are just starting to figure out that data is useful, let alone have a consolidated plan and data warehouse to move forward. This is a problem.

How can we catapult, or leapfrog, forward to a place where all data is prepared for usage? The logical data warehouse consultant in me says that there is no way to do that. It is a required part of the process that each data source and data point be managed and governed. It's critical that the *extract, transform, and load (ETL)* process be held in the highest regard, and there are no "easy" buttons for preparing and visualizing your data for users. Yet the data warehouse industry is rapidly evolving to allow for things like semantic-driven ETL, virtual storage, and modified architecture that makes the traditional data warehouse nothing but a pit stop on the data-train express.

In order to take advantage of these new technologies and methodologies, healthcare has to do something that it has never done before. It has to be an early adopter. I know what I am proposing. I've been in healthcare for 15 years; none of that time has been as an early adopter. I have worked in organizations that have been "fast followers"; I've also worked in plenty that are clearly "laggards." When it comes to data, healthcare is not reaching for the edge to see how sharp it is;

we are waiting, often for too long, for others to dull the blade. The organizations that have taken the leap of faith (into business intelligence [BI]) have found fantastic results and surmountable challenges.

GO BOLDLY

Forget everything you've read about traditional data warehouse best practices, including much of what I've told you. Don't concern yourself with comparing your maturity to other healthcare organizations. You should start, today, by comparing yourself to retail and financial services organizations. Don't simply settle for reports or dashboards; lead your organization toward the light. This means that we have to take bold steps toward a new reality—where data provides valuable insight to our organizations, and it does it in real time (or near real time). In order to do that we will have to start with the repository that provides the information that we need. We have to start with your data warehouse.

DISRUPTIVE TECHNOLOGIES

In my first book, *Healthcare Business Intelligence*, I talked a lot about the realities of getting data into a warehouse, not just from a data acquisition perspective, but also from a data modeling perspective. These areas continue to carry a degree of importance that we can't ignore. The only other way that we can achieve a data-driven healthcare organization (DDHO) is with very smart data scientists, and there is a huge gap in the availability of that skill set. Even if you had a team of 200 data scientists, the scalability of that scenario is unruly at best. Empowering a broader user base through easily accessible and contextually driven data is the way forward. But the exercise of getting data in and then back out in this way has confounded very smart people for decades. Thankfully, some disruptive technologies are now available that allow organizations to do just that—get data in as fast as possible, explore relationships, and create a model for broader usage.

When I think about truly disruptive technologies in this space, I need them to do certain things:

1. Integrate structured, semi-structured, and unstructured data from many disparate systems, because that's exactly what healthcare is.
2. Do it very quickly.
3. Be on a stable environment that allows for sophisticated security measures.
4. Be cost effective enough for the majority of healthcare organizations to take advantage of it, not just the big guys.
5. Provide contextual data in a highly consumable format to encourage self-service.

So, better, faster, cheaper, and more secure than anything else that's been introduced in the last 20 years—that would be disruptive.

HADOOP, THE CLOUD, AND MODERN DATA PLATFORMS

The word *Hadoop* entered my world about three years ago. Descriptive it is not; it reminds me of when my sister and I were talking about this new band we really liked. When our mother overheard us mention Bon Jovi she said, "Is that some kind of new pizza?" What is Hadoop? Descriptions vary, but simply it is the file management system that allows for rapid data acquisition through *tagging* data. Very much how Google works behind the scenes, Hadoop allows you to pull all kinds of structured, semi-structured, and unstructured data into these "files" and tag them with keywords such as "MRN" for Medical Record Number. Many new healthcare products are using Hadoop as a back end system, allowing them to rapidly acquire data and push it back out through varying user interfaces without the integration step or needing a developer to apply the business rules. The simplest use case is to allow a hospital to pull in their electronic health record data and use a semantic search to find all patients complaining of chest pains who are not on a statin. It's a powerful use case. Its rapid turnaround and open-source system is tempting, but it doesn't meet one of our most important criteria; it leaves out the need for contextual data in a highly visualized manner. It's just the back end that churns through data, tags it, and stores it in files for simple queries. But it's a start.

The *cloud*—where do I begin? Some healthcare organizations have run to the cloud with wild abandon, adopting it with the anticipation of huge cost savings and reduced need for infrastructure redundancy. I think most experts agree that the return on investment is still being worked out. But more than that, the security of the cloud is so confounding. Could you imagine explaining to your patient that her data was potentially accessed and when she asked you where her data actually was, you weren't able to answer? It was not because you didn't want to but because you didn't know. The cloud and the surrounding technologies have improved a great deal. The good news is that there are some vendors that have specialized in healthcare and are HIPAA compliant. The performance concerns of accessing data in a cloud are getting better, too, although that still has a ways to go. In my first book, I recommended that you skip the cloud for a while, in favor of keeping your data tucked in safely, exactly where you can physically access it. In just two short years, so many organizations are dealing with such large volumes of data that a critical review of the cloud is now warranted. Look for a vendor that specializes in healthcare, knows your state regulations, and is (of course) HIPAA compliant.

Modern data platforms are evolving all the time. In the grand scheme of things, data warehousing as an industry has been slow to adopt new strategies beyond the standard Inmon-versus-Kimball argument because regardless of your data modeling preferences, they work. Slight modifications that allow for a more agile approach to data warehousing (seemingly better aligned to Kimball than Inmon) have made a big splash and rightly so. But the fundamental way we access data hasn't really changed in the last 30 years. We take it out of our source systems, apply business rules, and put it somewhere for a BI product to access it. Done and done. Hadoop has changed this somewhat, although you can't really plug in a traditional BI product on top of that. *Semantic ETL*, a method of consuming data based on the actual data itself, is promising (connecting data based on keywords or terms in the data). Not much is known about many of these methods in terms of healthcare, which makes adoption challenging.

THE NEW WAY FORWARD

Although many of these new technologies are still untested, they are our best ways forward. Reflecting back on what it would mean to be a disruptive technology in healthcare, combining these key pieces—Hadoop, the cloud, and semantic ETL—gets us there faster than any other option we have available today. Of course, there are risks with anything new, but if we apply our RISE (reduce, identify, streamline, evaluate) model to the implementation of these efforts, we should be able to control the worst risks and take advantage of the best these combined systems have to offer.

> *The modern data platform (MDP) structure fits the disruptive technology definition and because it's designed to support analytics and reporting, it can really shine in healthcare.*
>
> —John O'Brien, Principal and CEO, Radiant Advisors

In Figure 4.1, there are three separate layers in the MDP that together operate to balance flexibility against rigidity. In Tier One, it is

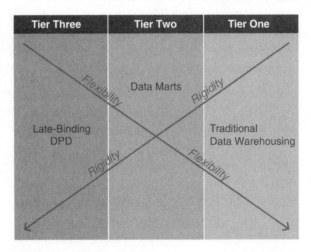

Figure 4.1 Modern Data Platform

everything data warehousing was before, or is now, with traditional *master data management* and very rigid and controlled methods and rules to create a "single source of truth."

In Tier Two we use an optimized platform (such as Netezza or Paraccel) in order of magnitude bigger, to create an analytics platform with large amounts of different types of event data and join reference data (the data warehouse) for attribution. This tier provides a much more sophisticated method of supporting analytics in a healthcare organization. It's structured to scale and provide support for *online analytic processing (OLAP)*.

Finally, there is Tier Three, the Hadoop-like layer. This is where we deviate drastically from the traditional healthcare information environment of the past. It is a schema-less dump of the data. It seems contrary to logic, but in this layer we don't worry about what the data looks like; we just bring in the data. This is what is generally referred to as late-binding. Why is that so important? Historically, the challenge with data warehouses, particularly in healthcare, was that we had to define all of the relationships in the data right away. That meant that we had to explore all the sources and know how patient A is related to doctor B is related to facility C, plus all associated attributes (i.e., patient A is diabetic, doctor B is an endocrinologist, and facility C has specific ratings for managing diabetic care). Defining all of those relationships and attributes slowed the process drastically. By the time we got the data, we had already moved on to another question or challenge. The technology has advanced so much that it's possible to use systems to identify certain relationships based on keywords or terms. Simply, the system (Hadoop, e.g.) pulls data in and tags it much like you and I do with a Word document. We name it something that will allow us to remember or connect it to something else. All of these tags then can be related to one another. But it doesn't do that on the front end; it does in late in the data acquisition process, hence the term *late binding*. But you do have a trade-off; you trade off the consistent, repeatable definitions that are the hallmark of a traditional data warehouse. That's what makes the MDP so compelling, because it balances the flexibility and volatility of Tier Three with the rigidity of data warehouse. The trade-off is worth it to get data in faster.

REDUCE THE UNKNOWNS

There are a lot of unknowns in some of these methods. Let's start with the impact of using Hadoop as discussed and what that could mean for reporting using a traditional dimension model. What if your population health team kept running the statin example above from the Hadoop-based system. Then they got a report from the dimensional model (the goal as always is to be the source of truth for data in the organization). The primary risk we run in this scenario is the potential to have differences in the data reported between the file system in Hadoop and the traditional reporting system. We can help manage the risk by modifying the tagging in Hadoop to ensure it's the most accurate representation of chest pains. To take best advantage of the late binding while still controlling the risk, we have to evolve governance through an agile approach.

IDENTIFY THE ALTERNATIVES

First, there is always the option to do nothing. We can either continue to manage the data the way that we've always done it, with a focus on reporting rather than analytics, or we just simply do nothing (with the hope that this focus on data goes away).

Second, we can do it the old-fashioned way, with the traditional data warehouse approach. But as we started this chapter, we defined disruptive technologies. Anyone reading this book probably is seriously considering or already has decided to become a data-driven organization. If that's true, then you don't have the luxury of doing nothing or trying it the way that you've always done it. It's time for healthcare to lead the charge, not wait for someone else. These are the alternatives, and they aren't that appealing.

STANDARDIZE

Standards are a common theme throughout this book. Regardless of when you bind the data, in order to create a truly broad adoption of data, we have to make sure that we apply some level of standard to the data so that everyone sees the same answer to the same question, or at least the answer is similar enough that most business users are comfortable with the difference. The trade-off on rigidity for the MDP can seem tough at first, but remember Tier One is still your traditional data warehouse from which most of your business users will access data.

In order to standardize your data in the MDP, you will have to change how your data governance group works. First, the group will have to start to decide where data should live and whether certain data elements move between tiers. In some cases the answer will always be yes, but in other cases they might challenge the platform. For example, let's extend our scenario, where we run a query to determine how many of our patients who were not on a statin had chest pains. We briefly discussed the potential that the query run out of Tier Three (Hadoop-like layer) could differ from a report run out of Tier One. This is an example where the question you ask needs to be:

- Answered quickly.
- Consistently answered to best manage your population.

Therefore, that data needs to move between tiers and should be tightly managed and coupled to ensure that the difference is manageable. But what if your question is: "Of the patients who had chest pains but were not on a statin, how many are presenting with multiple complaints?" You certainly want that question to be answered quickly, because you are likely trying to get to comorbidities and access effectiveness of your emergency department triage method (as an example). But do you need to consistently get that information to best manage your population? Or could you always get that data from Tier Three and never formally report on it through Tier One? These are the kinds of questions your data governance group will have to ask themselves as they adjust to a new way of managing data. Not all data needs to live in all three tiers; let it live where it makes sense based on the type of data and usage.

EVALUATE AND IMPROVE

Here's the most important attribute of our RISE model for the MDP. Because so much of it is new and untested, we have to be ready, willing, and able to make midcourse corrections. Early in your adoption of

MDP, the team should identify stage gates, logical places to stop in the development cycle to ensure that whatever you're building is going to work. That doesn't mean that you can just kill the project when things start to get a little tense (and they will get tense), but it does allow a modicum of control over some of the bigger investment pieces like Hadoop or an optimized platform investment. If you already have a traditional data warehouse and a data governance group, you're ahead of the game. Rely on your data governance group to help identify some of the questions or scenarios that would work best in a late-binding scenario. Then do a pilot test of the Hadoop-like layer. Don't connect it to anything yet; run these test scenarios and see how close they get to the answer that you would expect. If it's really far off, then make some adjustments and try again. As a team, continue to check in with one another to determine if you're comfortable moving forward based on the goal of late binding. In other words, don't compare the Hadoop-like system to a traditional data warehouse; remember that you are trying to balance the trade-off of fast and perfect.

Next, do the same for the analytic layer. You can't really be a DDHO without a solid analytic layer to support the depth of questions that healthcare has. We have so much data that an investment in an optimized platform (such as Teradata or Netezza) makes sense for most healthcare organizations. This will be an important stage gate for the project, and one that should take some serious time and commitment from your analysts. Once you make your decision as to which platform you're comfortable with (even if that is just the SQL server for now), it's time to manage the data between the tiers.

Rely on a full end-to-end test of the system by creating a set of use cases for each tier. These use cases should include queries and reports that would require the data to meet certain pre-determined standards before moving between tiers. This will help you confirm the user scenarios of each tier and determine the variance of acceptable data between each of the layers. The variance will be key in determining how much exposure you provide to certain user groups to each of the layers. In other words, if you know that the late-binding third tier is consistently off from your traditional data warehouse in the first tier by 10 percent, many business users will be uncomfortable with that degree of variance. But if the use case is to quickly identify a population set, maybe a variance of 10 percent is manageable for that use case.

The best way to think about this is to understand your user continuum. I wrote about this in my first book, and I've adapted it here to explain how different users may access different tiers. (See Figure 4.2.)

The better you understand your population set, the easier time you will have accessing what data moves and what data stays based on the use case. Continue to evaluate the data, use cases, and the project overall to ensure that you can make key corrections in approach. When you do that aggressively, keeping in mind the goal of disruptive technologies, you will be able to deliver the best possible scenario for your organization.

THE FUTURE IS NOW

After many conversations with people way smarter than me, this is the model that came out the winner. Some organizations are already doing this, so you won't be the first, but you also won't be the last, and that's an important place to *not* be. The future is scary. I have a six-year-old who keeps asking me what will happen when the world will end. Will the Sun go away? Will the Earth crumble below our feet? They seem like really existential questions for a six-year-old (the result of watching *The Croods* too many times). No one knows the future, but I believe that controlling what you do know makes the unknown bearable. What we do know is our data. We know that it's messy, and unstructured, and an absolute gold mine if managed correctly.

We know our industry; it's challenged right now, but the goal is still the same. We need to provide the best care possible to improve the quality of life. We know that we have to make money to keep our doors open, not a very popular fact but true nonetheless.

We know that we have to improve. We are the only country in the world that spends as much as we do in terms of life expectancy, only to get an average return (for simplicity's sake, I will avoid the inevitable conversation about the food industry). I'm not okay with the fact that my son's generation is the first one that will live fewer years than their parents. We have to improve.

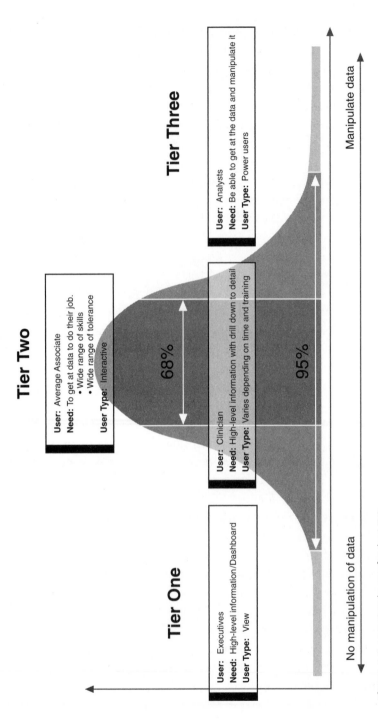

Tier One

User: Executives
Need: High-level information/Dashboard
User Type: View

Tier Two

User: Average Associate
Need: To get at data to do their job.
  • Wide range of skills
  • Wide range of tolerance
User Type: Interactive

Tier Three

User: Analysts
Need: Be able to get at the data and manipulate it
User Type: Power users

User: Clinician
Need: High-level information with drill down to detail
User Type: Varies depending on time and training

68%

95%

No manipulation of data

Manipulate data

Figure 4.2 User Continuum for the MDP

If these are all the things we know, then we can take what is important to us here and use it as fuel to take the leap of faith toward a new future in healthcare BI—a future where data lives in multiple places, and we manage it to ensure quality and consistency. But that doesn't get in the way of getting data fast and answers faster.

CHAPTER 5

Creating a Data-Driven Healthcare Organization

L ast year, as we were working through some marketing content for 2013, we were discussing how to categorize the work that I do. It's not as easy as it sounds. I'm not a technologist; I can't come in and develop a report or write some code for data acquisition. The work that I do most appropriately falls under "soft skills." I help organizations figure out what they want to do with their data and how they can achieve that in the most cost-effective, fastest way possible. We discussed a few specific scenarios, and then our marketing manager said to me, "You're like a data therapist." It stuck.

For years business intelligence (BI) consultants ignored the organizational transformation that had to take place. It felt too much like management consulting, and most BI consultants are recovering information technology (IT) professionals. Carving out a niche in this area and, more important, showing the importance and value of the effort, took years. Thankfully, most healthcare organizations intuitively understood the undertaking and have continued to articulate the reasons why it's so important. Becoming a successful data-driven healthcare organization (DDHO) requires balancing people, process, culture, and technology.

Transforming the culture and creating an organizational structure that can support business intelligence is always a hot topic when I talk with a client. The trouble here is that we aren't creating a traditional BI team; we're making a cultural shift toward data-driven decisions. That requires a completely different perspective as to how to align the organization.

We defined in Chapter 2 the data-driven healthcare organization. It's highly dependent on one thing: *action*. That means that however we organize our efforts around data-driven decisions, it has to focus on the action as a result of the insight.

Here are three things a data-driven organization needs to do organizationally to ensure success:

1. Make organizational structure changes to encourage data sharing and management.
2. Train business users to become more savvy data consumers.
3. Readjust data governance rules.

Training business users and readjusting governance seems relatively straightforward; where the challenge presents itself is how to align organizationally to become a true DDHO. I'm often asked if BI organizations should be consolidated under a broader organizational umbrella or decentralized into independent business units to spread the word of data. There is no right or wrong way to do this, and it greatly depends on the structure and willingness of your organization to make significant change. But, in general, the healthcare companies I've seen are relatively immature at BI and very matrixed, which makes change on this scale exceedingly difficult. Therefore, a federated or consolidated organization in the enterprise is your best chance to succeed as you begin the journey; but you can't forget that because of the matrix approach, having resources throughout the organization will help drive change through the enterprise.

Air traffic control uses a hub-and-spoke methodology to ensure that traffic is managed—essentially passing a plane from hub to spoke and back. If it's good enough to keep planes in the air and in motion, it could probably work for an organizational structure that will be highly reliant on the need for action. This hub-and-spoke approach will help you manage the centralized aspect to have better management of standards but create repeatable frameworks to disperse throughout the organization. (See Figure 5.1.)

The center of this hub-and-spoke model is an information-enabling team. Their primary directive is to create standards and provide support to the organization. Requests or questions come into the hub and answers, standards, and support come out of the hub to the spokes, or different parts of the organization. Ideally, you would have resources that formally report through the hub that actually work alongside the spokes. The goal is to align to the expertise that resides in the spokes (i.e., financial analysts stay in finance) but partner with the BI and analytics professionals who work in the hub. Your hub resources can stay focused on support, standards, data governance, data architecture, data acquisition, and integration. All department-specific analysts stay in the spoke but have a formal (or informal) reporting relationship with the hub.

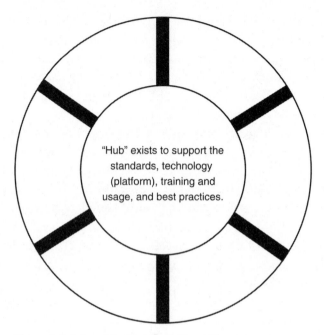

Figure 5.1 Hub-and-Spoke Organizational Structure

IT OR THE BUSINESS?

It's time to address the stickiest situation we have in healthcare BI: the relationship between IT and the business. At the 2013 Healthcare BI Summit in September, we had an open-networking event. During this event the majority of the attendees described their relationship with IT as being their biggest barrier. This is not acceptable; we have too many barriers outside of our organizations to be dealing with barriers we create inside our own organization. I've always been a strong advocate for BI staying in the business. I firmly believe that alignment is the only long-term way to success, but that is jeopardized when IT and business aren't formally aligned or the business side is not empowered and staffed to deliver. If this situation sounds familiar, I encourage you to address it head-on before trying to tackle the next step on your data-driven journey. These relationships and structures can take a toll on your staff, who often feel that they work and work and never please the business (IT) or facilitate, organize, and prioritize to never please IT (business).

Now, if you're serious about taking your organization to the next level, this will be a controversial next step: All information-based tasks should report up through a chief data officer (CDO) who reports directly to the chief executive officer (CEO). That's right—there is no formal reporting relationship to the chief information officer (CIO) or the IT organization. The only exception to that rule is when your CIO is truly keyed in to the information aspect of your organization (and such CIOs do exist). Most CIOs struggle with this under the weight of electronic medical records (EMRs) and infrastructure because it is a fundamentally different skill set. Aligning it this way takes the best advantage of key skill sets.

CHIEF DATA OFFICER: JOB DESCRIPTION

The CDO leads all information-based tasks and is responsible for the data strategy, governance, and data evangelism throughout the enterprise. The CDO is part of the executive team and reports to the CEO. The CDO is tasked with operationalizing the data-driven vision of the organization through management of people, process, and technology.

Responsibilities will include:

- Developing a plan to ensure high usability of data
- Using technology as a method to deliver information value
- Aligning to key business units within the enterprise (i.e., quality improvement)
- Leading the architectural standards of data
- Budget responsibility
- Developing a team of data practitioners to enable and support a culture of data sharing and repurposing, including data scientists, data quality experts, and data architects
- Aligning to internal and external healthcare data standards
- Balancing the technical with the business needs

The ideal candidate will have experience in healthcare data management, with increasing responsibilities for staffing and return on investment. (See Figure 5.A.)

(Continued)

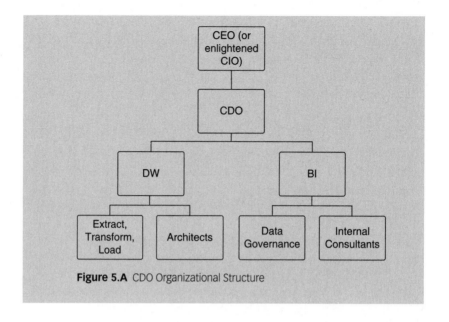

Figure 5.A CDO Organizational Structure

Doing these two things, creating a hub-and-spoke model and aligning all information-based activities under a CDO, will position your organization to use the information it's distributing and put the responsibility of getting content out to the business users in a streamlined, buck-stops-here structure. The goal is to remove the barriers of statements such as: "I need the ETL [extract, transform, load] updated, and IT is too busy," or "I don't know what to build because the business hasn't given me the requirements."

As I was thinking about this structure, trying to anticipate the impact of each particular scenario, I had an enlightened conversation with Charles Boicey, the Informatics Solutions Architect at the University of California, Irvine. It turns out that this is exactly how UC Irvine has structured all of their traditional BI and data warehouse functions. Even though he reports to the CIO, Mr. Boicey is responsible for all of the aspects of data and information from requirements to architecture, acquisition to analytics. Mr. Boicey is a true data scientist; he started his career as a registered nurse and found his way to computer science because it was "interesting." UC Irvine is ahead of the game; after having adopted EMRs in the late 1980s, they recognized the need for better information to business users. It took them a while, but today they are tackling the big questions and anticipating rather than reacting to the latest challenges (such as social media, natural language processing, and mobile technologies) and regulatory requirements.

TRAINING

Once you've created a new organizational structure that will be able to advance your organization's data maturity you have to prepare your organization for consuming and using data. This is a very different exercise than training business users on software. Now we have to train business users how to think about data in a more critical and thoughtful way. The ideal scenario is that everyone in your organization, from the CEO down to the receptionist, understands the key performance indicators that drive the business and their personal role in that success.

Years ago, when I started at Lancet, one of the first things that I was shown was the company financials. It was explained to me in terms that a brand-new consultant could understand. I had a direct and immediate impact on the bottom line, and therefore the success of the company and my peers. In many ways that was a much simpler view of data than in a healthcare organization, but it was equally powerful. Everyone understands how it works, and we are given all the information every month to ensure that we are as up to date as anyone else in the organization. This data-driven approach saved Lancet years ago, when their biggest client disappeared overnight due to an acquisition. The next day, rather than packing up their boxes, every consultant became a salesperson. When you empower your staff to use information to better your business, the results can be revolutionary.

WHAT AND HOW SHOULD WE TEACH?

The culture of any industrialized society is suffused with quantitative information. Some quantitative messages are simple and direct; others involve a relatively complicated process of inference. Knowing how to think about statistics makes possible the comprehension of both kinds of messages.

—John L. Phillips, Jr., *How to Think about Statistics*, 5th ed.

The best way to approach training is to create a series of course-ware that your business users can access when it's convenient for them. That means it has to be in many different formats. It will take a bit longer to create, but the value will pay dividends in the long run.

In my first few years in college I competed in public speaking. I had a coach who taught us one thing about the content we were to present, regardless of whether it was about nuclear fusion or how to cook a ham-burger (a presentation I actually made): "Keep it simple, stupid" (KISS). That acronym has fallen out of favor in our more politically correct times but the lesson is still as valuable. Not everyone intuitively understands data or is even interested in it. The more we complicate it, the worse position we will be in. The success of a DDHO relies heavily on everyone in the organization rallying around the battle cry of "I make data-driven decisions." If they don't have the right tools to do that, then it doesn't really matter how much data you have or how great it is.

The curriculum for training your average business user will look a lot like the Stats 101 class that most first-year college students are required to take. The important distinction is that your training should be very specific to your organization and the key performance metrics that your executives and board of directors have identified. The most important thing you can focus on for the content is to teach them *how* to think about statistics, not *what* to think. It's an incredibly important distinction and aligns well with visualizing data.

Your first set of content should address descriptive statistics, or the measures of central tendency. You can include things like confidence intervals and the importance of populations and sampling as well. Then you want to take it to the next level by addressing correlations, trends, and regression. These are used heavily in healthcare research and your staff should be well versed in the ins and outs. As you get to the more advanced stages of statistics, such as analysis of variance, you can start to reduce the number of staff that are required to know and understand this content. Beyond these basics, some of your analysts may want or need to seek out additional training. Finally, you should provide a number of sessions regarding visualizing data. It should be clear to every staff member how to read all graph types and when a graph is inappropriately representing data.

GOVERNING DATA FOR OUR NEW MODERN DATA PLATFORM

Updating your governance structure has as much to do with your new data platform as it has to do with your new organizational structure. I help organizations with governance a lot. It seems to be the one area that stalls information distribution. When you align your DDHO under the new role of CDO, some of those organic organizational barriers disappear. In their place, though, a new set of challenges arise as a result of the late-binding data repository in the Tier One structure of our new *modern data platform (MDP)*. As you may recall from Chapter 4, the first tier of our new platform is a large data repository taking advantage of the new Hadoop-like technologies. We have traded off some of the rigidity of a data warehouse for the immediacy of just getting the data where we can grab it. The first question we get when we do that is "What about data quality?" It's a fair concern; in order to get quick access to data, we have to be willing to trade off some control. By applying RISE (reduce, identify, streamline, evaluate), we can and should reduce the unknowns of this particular concern. Allowing access to data should be limited to a specified user set and through a specific set of products. Our hub-and-spoke model reassures us that the right people throughout the organization will still get timely access to the data without the barriers of traditional data warehouse rigidity or the risk of releasing information that lacks context. Combining the best of technology with the right people and process limits risk and aligns for better information usage.

The second tier of our new MDP is where traditional data marts live. This is where an analytics sandbox would reside, allowing access from analysts. Most healthcare organizations have some version of an analytic sandbox that works. The question is about how much you should govern the "analytic" aspect of the sandbox and the content that comes out of it. Procedurally, you have to find a way to take advantage of the innovation that comes from an analytic layer and the resources that access that data. You don't want to stifle the incredible wealth of information and efficiencies that can come from the analytic layer, so you let the analysts self-govern the tier. In traditional organizational structures, where BI and IT resided in different organizations (and analysts were flung out into the far reaches of the organization), the fear of allowing self-governing of the analytics sandbox usually made both BI and IT managers look at me like I was crazy. Our new organizational structure aligns that well and removes the barrier.

Finally, we are to Tier Three, the traditional data warehouse, where we are comfortable governing data. Not much changes here from the way that we've always governed data; it just happens to be a little easier because organizationally we are better aligned to do it. You will also know a lot more about your data prior to its reaching the data warehouse because of the previous layers that most data will go through. I predict that as healthcare organizations get used to moving data through these separate environments, the need for the traditional data warehouse will ebb.

We will continue to formally adopt data definitions, identify data quality parameters, and solve for data quality questions and concerns for this tier. Where appropriate, some of that structure may be pushed up through the first tier to ensure data consistency. In other words, our example of looking for all patients who present in our emergency department with symptoms of cardiac arrest without being on a statin could benefit from standard definitions of *patient, cardiac arrest,* and certain statin classes. In the analytic layer, we could go a step further and, using the same standard definitions, look for certain factors that could predict issues, such as age, weight, smoking, high blood pressure, and cholesterol management. Someday, we may even be able to use behavioral data, such as genetic indicators, to isolate those patients whom we should be managing more proactively (or more aggressively). But we must always remember that Tiers Three and Two are meant to be less managed, so while you can always improve consistency and data usage, you can't get in the way of getting information into business users' hands.

This chapter is jam-packed with revolutionary recommendations. If they feel unreachable and perhaps a bit too drastic, just take one step that seems attainable. Many of these recommendations require a level of maturity that your organization may not yet have. That's okay; it takes time. Start with realigning your organization to the hub-and-spoke model. Then start doing analysis into the Hadoop-like structures we discussed in Chapter 4. In Chapter 6, there are a few tips as to how to adapt to our new big data reality that may be helpful as well.

Some of this may take some time to adjust to. I remember watching *Oprah* a number of years ago and the author Eckhart Tolle was on. He was talking about his new book, *A New Earth*. He said, in so many words, that most people won't understand it, and that's okay. You're just not ready. I suddenly remembered that fifth-grade math teacher who told me that I shouldn't ask so many questions about math, because I was a girl and wouldn't be good at it anyway. I was offended, as if someone had just patted me on the head and said, "Don't worry your pretty little head." So I promptly went out and bought the Tolle book and was absolutely determined to not only understand it but dismiss it as junk. Guess what happened? I read 40 pages, declared it impossible, and put it away. I haven't touched it since. The truth is I wasn't ready. I'm still not sure I am. I can't even tell you what the book is about. You may feel similarly, as you read some of these ideas, that perhaps you or your organization isn't ready. But, what we're trying to do here, you and I, is re-create healthcare with data. Yes, the ideas may seem drastic to some, obvious to others, but most important they are doable and critical to be successful.

CHAPTER **6**

Applying Big Data to Change Healthcare

At the risk of sounding completely out of the loop or flat-out crazy, there is no such thing as "big data." Unfortunately, thanks to the trends driven in the business intelligence (BI) marketplace, I'm asked to talk about "big data" a lot. Let's start with how you define "big data" (and yes, I'm using the quotation marks on purpose). The most broadly accepted definition isn't really a definition at all but attributes of the data, such as "volume, velocity, and variety." So, if you take that literally, we've always had "big data"; we've always had data that came in faster than we could consume it, at volumes that we didn't (or chose not to) integrate and with the variety that was beyond our reach.

I've worked with a lot of healthcare organizations and not one of them is actually *using* "big data." I started asking around to those vendors that talk about "big data" and asked them to bring to bear case studies of organizations actively using "big data"; I got crickets. I'm not saying that it *doesn't* exist; I just can't *prove* that it does. It's like the Loch Ness Monster or Bigfoot. I say this in jest, sort of. I attempted to contact many organizations inside and outside of my network. In many cases they expressed interest but never returned a phone call or email to my follow-up requests. It could be that many of these organizations just didn't want to talk about what they were doing for the obvious competitive differentiation that it could introduce. That's a fair assertion, and I'm willing to give them the benefit of the doubt. But where does that leave us? My initial intent for this chapter was to use these case studies as a blueprint for recommendations to other healthcare organizations. I've been fortunate to have had some illuminating conversations with organizations like UC Irvine and Premier, which have informed many of the recommendations that are outlined in these pages.

UC Irvine's Approach to "Big Data"

PROFILE

My conversation with UC Irvine was enlightening, and only toward the end of the call did we actually start to talk about big data. Much of the call was directed toward how they've organized themselves to be able to take advantage of "big data," and those recommendations are in Chapter 4.

(Continued)

(Continued)

But make no mistake: UC Irvine is using big data, and even starting to figure out the last frontier of unstructured data. Their focus is on improved outcomes, and I plan to watch very closely to see how they do.

I think it's important that we first agree on a definition of "big data" in healthcare, and what it can and most important *cannot* do for us. It's not without risk, and the RISE (reduce, identify, streamline, evaluate) model encourages us to identify the risks so we can identify alternatives. I'll give you the "volume, velocity, and variety" attributes of big data; many people (including myself) have introduced the need to identify *value* in the data, regardless of the volume or velocity. What "big data" really represents is a diverse and persistent stream of data that presents challenges associated with performance, management, and storage. It offers us an opportunity to utilize a population of whatever you are interested in measuring. In healthcare that's a powerful advantage, if it can be harnessed. Now, more than ever, we have the opportunity to manage our patient and member population by representing them as they exist, not as they statistically may be. The rare comorbidities now have an opportunity to be tracked, managed, and monitored like those that are much better known. This is a powerful and sometimes provocative proposition. If you could just manage your "big data," you would suddenly be able to harness the power of hundreds of years of experience and magically cure the weak and sick. "Big data" has yet to deliver on that compelling case study with any consistency. It's important here to make the distinction between case studies that are well known and prolific versus the average organization's BI maturity, ability, and experience. Organizations like UPMC have been doing this for years; they've created an organization that revolves around and supports data. For the rest of us, who are just dipping our toes into data warehousing and BI, the ability to use "big data" is a lot like the fishing stories my dad used to tell. There is some basis of fact, but the likelihood is remote.

One important distinction that should be made at this point is the difference between the data itself, the systems we use to support it, and the methods we use to support it. Often, in the popular marketing content that is available today, those three things are referred to interchangeably, and I am here to tell you they are *not* interchangeable.

First, let's talk about the data itself. There's a difference between the data type (structured, semi-structured, and unstructured), frequency (how often your data is updated), and then of course the volume of data, the sheer size. Much of the talk about "big data" is addressing the type, but the products that have been created actually address the volume. One would argue that you can't talk about one without the other, but the organizations I've talked with found good value in using the products to address performance because of the volume of the data. In other research, some express concerns about the performance of these systems when you use large volume of unstructured data. In other words, if you just have a whole lot of data that is highly structured, the products that are available can easily improve performance. They aren't as good at handling large volumes of *unstructured* data. That may have more to do with the way that the data itself exists (think of it as a large file system with tags on it), so the methodologies in which we model and support the data are important but evolving rapidly.

THE CALL OF BIG DATA

As I write this, early in 2014, big data is in its infancy. It has its supporters and detractors. I'm not sure where I fall on that continuum yet, as the research I've done tells me that there is still a lot to learn. I've been in the data warehousing/business intelligence business for 15 years and what I know for sure is that there is no magic bullet. The work is the work. Adding insane volumes of diverse data hardly makes that job easier. The concern I have is that, as a healthcare industry, we aren't very good at traditional data warehousing and as I've said before, we have to leapfrog our maturity to move forward. We can't do that if we're trying to adapt to a very immature "big data" market at the same time.

Let's be clear about something—"big data" is here to stay. It sort of pains me to say that. I say it because of the forward-thinking and compelling ideas I've found while researching this book. *Natural language processing (NLP)* is the future of "big data," but even that's evolving to include ontology-based data management (OBDM), as referenced in a blog entry on the Association for Computing Machinery: Special Interest Group on Management of Data site, "The OBDM," created to address the fact "that governing the resources (data, metadata, services, processes, etc.) of modern information systems is still an outstanding problem" (Lenzerini, 2013). Managing these modern information systems, and the corresponding "big data" that goes with them, seems to require a new way of thinking.

Traditional data warehouse practices are functional but will not scale to the volumes of data that we are clearly heading toward. In a traditional data warehouse approach, we spend an inordinate amount of time on the front end beating data into submission so the average user can consume it on the back end. For most projects, that portion of the effort takes up approximately 80 percent of the time. Now imagine that multiplied by hundreds of data sources with increasing data volumes. Forget server scalability; *people* don't have that scalability. Context-driven or semantic-driven data acquisition becomes a reality. This starts to feel very *Star Trek*-y, but the future is much closer than we realize, as noted in a recent article in *Information Management* titled "The Analytic Trifecta," where you apply a semantic layer through the data abstraction layer allowing for a common repository and a location to manage data governance efforts (Ryan, 2014).

> *The future of Big Data is neither structured nor unstructured. Big Data will be structured by intuitive methods (i.e., "genetic algorithms"), or using inherent patterns that emerge from the data itself and not from rules imposed on data sets by humans.*
>
> —Marc Maxson (2013)

Historically, as we've applied the data warehouse standards, we've applied an existing mental model of the data on the front end, and not letting the data speak for itself. That was required because our systems and even our skill sets were not able to make sense from the chaos.

You've heard the old adage, "The whole is greater than the sum of its parts." Well, the "whole" is big data, but we keep applying "parts"-type thinking to its management. As the "big data" maturity improves, we will be able to program these "smart" algorithms to data in the near future (Maxson, 2013).

EVOLVE OR DIE

We've established that there are very few strong case studies of regular healthcare organizations using "big data." That can't stop us. Our world has changed entirely too much for us to wait to be a fast follower; it's time to evolve or die. That doesn't mean we have to be reckless about our approach; we can be assertive in our approach, just mindful of the risks and opportunities. Before we go too far I have to find a way to refer to "big data" without the quotes. You may be saying to yourself, "Okay, Laura, just use big data or BD, what's the 'big' deal?" The "big" deal (at least to me) is that "big data" is forever and inextricably linked to marketing fluff. I don't work in marketing fluff. I work in real-world scenarios that can help healthcare organizations decide how to best proceed. In order for me to frame up this work and make recommendations, it has to be clear that this is about data that is diverse, persistent, and powerful but absolutely 100 percent real, *usable*, and tangible. Otherwise, I'm no better than all the others out there trying to get a leg up (I'm not any better, but that's an existential issue, not a DW/BI issue).

When my son was about three years old, he started understanding words and phrases in a much more tangible way. As a result my husband and I had to come up with a code system so we could discuss our plans without ramping up our three-year-old. Our code system was simple; we referred to something by a proper name, for example, we called the zoo (one of our favorite places to go) the "Howard." I've considered calling "big data" "Sophia" (a totally random selection, not after anyone in particular), but that just didn't seem right. In all seriousness, what you call something matters. That's why data governance is so important (more on that later). So I'm going to call "big data" *diverse persistent data (DPD)* from now on.

Table 6.1 DPD and RISE

Reduce the unknowns	What do data quality and data profiling mean in terms of DPD?
Identify the alternatives	We could not do it. Or we could wait for other organizations to do it that are similar to us.
Streamline standards	If the goal is faster, how can we change the certified data standards? Should we change them?
Evaluate	Determine one or two pilot projects to evaluate based on certain predetermined metrics.

DPD requires us to apply our RISE model from Chapter 2 to ensure that we can use the data without introducing any additional risk. Table 6.1 outlines some of the most obvious attributes of DPD associated with RISE.

LET'S ORGANIZE THIS AND TAKE ALL THE FUN OUT OF IT

For years there was a storage closet full of supplies in the copy room of the psychology department at UW-Stout that required a fast hand and a brave heart. It was a disaster; stuff was everywhere. Because of the lack of organization or inventory control, it was easy for students who worked for the professors to grab a sticky note or two (not that *I* ever did that) for personal use. I remember coming back one fall and the supply closet had been completely organized, with labels and everything. On the outside of that supply closet now was a cartoon, with two people standing over a mess and one proclaiming "Let's organize this and take all the fun out of it!" From chaos and frustration came reliability and predictability, and that's exactly what we have to find from DPD.

When talking with organizations that were *trying* DPD, a couple of attributes become immediately obvious. First, their IT maturity was much higher than that of the average healthcare organization. Two cases were peripheral healthcare organizations that provided support to payers and providers. One of their primary value-adds to their clients was to provide data, reporting, and analytics so clients could make more informed decisions. That prompted both organizations to be more aggressive in their approach to DPD. They are feeling the "evolve or die" right where it hits home, their book of business. If they didn't find a way to deliver better information to you, their customer, they would lose you as a client. Hospitals don't have that pressure point. If someone is hurt or ill, she isn't going to stop the ambulance to ask if the hospital has good reporting.

Another similarity was their user base. It was diverse and, in one case, very large. Thousands of users needed to access their system, pulling all kinds of data every day, every hour. That was putting an extreme amount of pressure on their systems, and performance degradation was a reality. Finally, and most obviously, was the data itself. No doubt, we are talking about data volumes that would have boggled our minds just a few years ago. If you added that to the number of users that needed to access it, you were looking at a perfect storm, one that traditional "big data" vendors could actually clearly deliver on.

It was interesting to me that in both cases they were using highly structured data, primarily billing and predefined flat files that clients sent to them. Moreover, these organizations are applying the RISE model without even realizing it. They are trying this new approach on their DPD in an area that is well understood and easily controlled: structured data. They can see a clear benefit through something that can be measured, like performance. Once they've mastered that, they're ready to turn to the next proof of concept. Premier is using semi-structured data in their DPD environment and having excellent results. In neither case, though, was the organization prepared to say that unstructured data was on their short list to try next.

▼ Premier Is Leading the Way in "Big Data"

PROFILE

Premier is a well-known healthcare improvement company. According to their website, "Premier members are pioneering collaborative efforts that transform healthcare." One of the ways health systems do this is by using the "PremierConnect" integrated technology platform, which combines patient data on one-in-four U.S. hospital discharges, evidence-based best practices from 2.5 million daily clinical transactions, and $40 billion

(*Continued*)

(Continued)

in annual provider purchases. Premier's "big data" efforts started with a pressure point —data volumes were increasing rapidly along with the number of customers utilizing their analytical systems. Premier's challenge was how to turn their customers' "big data" into "fast and actionable data" (i.e., how to reduce the cycle time from the receipt of data to actionable information).

Premier is an incredibly mature IT organization. When the new chief information officer joined, a number of key initiatives were started, including experimenting with "big data." There was some skepticism at first, but after going through the training, it became apparent to their most senior-level people that there was something compelling about the technology, and they decided to pursue some proof-of-concept (POC) activity. What we can learn from Premier is how to experiment intelligently, applying good decision making to our approach to DPD. After a number of POCs, Premier has decided that their future includes an infrastructure that aligns with DPD, improving performance and innovations cycle time.

I propose that you take a page out of Premier's book and start with training. Pick a couple of your senior developers and offer them the training that's provided by the "big data" vendors. Then outline the POC projects that you believe will provide an opportunity and value to the organization. Test, retest, evaluate, and adjust. When it becomes clear that the risk is small and the advantages are big, then and only then are you ready to start making full use of DPD. When I asked Tom Palmer and his team at Premier what some of their tips were, besides starting with training and POCs, they also recommended that you partner with the "big data" vendor. After all, right now there is no one who knows that product set better and what it's capable of.

DIPPING YOUR BIG TOE INTO BIG DATA

It's tempting to jump into the data lake. Healthcare has a lot of data, structured, semi-structured, and unstructured. Our use cases (the reasons that we need to use the data) are evolving and increasing every day. There is good reason to start to investigate DPD and its associated benefits for your organization.

REFERENCES

Lenzerini, M. (2013, May 14). "Ontology-Based Data Management." Retrieved March 3, 2014, from ACM Sigmod: http://wp.sigmod.org/?p=871.

Maxson, M. (2013, August). "The Future of Big Data Is Quasi-Structured." Retrieved March 3, 2014, from Chewy Chunks: http://chewychunks .wordpress.com/2013/03/23/future-of-big-data-structure/. Ryan, L. (2014, June 20). "The Analytic Trifecta: Abstraction, the Cloud and Visualization," Information Management. Retrieved

CHAPTER **7**

Making Data
Consumable

am currently in information overload. I feel overwhelmed with the speed and volume of data that comes at me every day. I have always prided myself on being up to date on impactful news stories and a few other topics that I have found fascinating, but lately I find myself just not as interested or, worse, only interested in the sound bites. Depth of knowledge doesn't seem to be as important today as breadth.

I'm not the only one. It seems like the whole world is in information overload these days. Part of the problem is we have so much information coming at us we're not able to pay attention to the information that is important. In order to become a data-driven healthcare organization (DDHO), we have to find a way to make sure that we provide the opportunities to present data so that our end users, from doctor to patient, know what's important and can take action on those few pieces of information.

Knowing what to pay attention to takes more focus than it should. The influx of "dashboards" into business intelligence (BI) initially offered an elegant way to visualize a lot of data quickly. As the pendulum swung the other way, we *dashboarded* everything, so much so that it's become a verb. Software vendors quickly jumped on the visualization bandwagon, some of them taking the time to research and work with experts in the field, others just providing bar graphs and pie graphs and calling it good enough. In order to take advantage of these new capabilities, we didn't adjust our staffing model or hire people who understood how to visualize data; we just let our developers do it. You know what we got? A proliferation of poorly designed data that can actually mislead you.

Now we have a lot of data, most of it poorly or inappropriately visualized, and we are expected to make more informed decisions from it. One important factor of being a data-driven organization is that it has to be action-oriented, and that's difficult to do when your data is pretty but doesn't tell you anything.

HOW WE PRESENT INFORMATION MATTERS

This is true regardless of the audience. Visually appealing data is one thing, and you could argue that the insanely popular "infographic" is an example of that. It's just pretty; it doesn't help you actually consume the information. It's a representation of information using graphics, like a graphic of a pill broken into sections to show the different population types that take a particular drug. It's a pretty way to present the data, and it likely sparks your brain in a slightly different way than just using a pie graph, but does it actually help you consume the information?

 ## WHAT IS AN *INFOGRAPHIC?*

Infographics are graphic visual representations of information, data, or knowledge intended to present complex information quickly and clearly. They can improve cognitions by utilizing graphics to enhance the human visual system's ability to see patterns and trends.

We can't argue that infographics are visual. But their ability to improve cognitions could be argued; I'm not sure how important it is that there is a pink stick figure and a blue stick figure to represent the gender diversity of a population. If nothing else, they make us pay attention, and vision does trump all of our other senses, taking up half of our brain's resources (Medina, 2008). Part of the problem with relying on vision, though, is that what we see is what our brain tells us, thereby leaving a lot open to interpretation. The function of vision is broken out into three separate activities, which are then brought back together. What we are doing is making sense out of chaos, using our brain as a contextual filter based on prior knowledge. This process is critical to understand as we begin our journey to appropriately visualizing data. Sometimes infographics can communicate information well; other times it's just a nice distraction or brochure filler.

What makes data consumable? That's a difficult question to answer. "I know it when I see it" certainly applies. It's easy to find data that isn't consumable; it's everywhere. Exploding pie charts, bar graphs, or line graphs with every color of the rainbow, the wrong data in the wrong graph. Visualized data is only part of what we should consider consumable data.

Many people have explored the idea of data visualization in a much deeper way than we will in this book. The important thing for us to recognize is that this is a discipline, with experts and standards. We will explore some of those here and in Appendix F.

Guiding Principles for Information Design

- Avoid acronyms.
- Don't use jargon.
- Stick with a monochromatic color scheme.
- Over-label content.
- Provide benchmarks as much as possible.
- Keep it simple.

As you're designing keep in mind that you are looking to provide *context, accessibility, and ease of use.*

> *Don't sacrifice accuracy in the name of coolness.*
> —Mike Erickson

WHEN WE PRESENT THE INFORMATION MATTERS, TOO

We talk a lot about how we visualize data but rarely about when. If we assume that being a DDHO requires action, presenting the data in a timely manner is critical to our ability to make decisions and respond in time to ensure that those decisions matter. I can't tell you how often I see healthcare organizations still making decisions from reports that are one, two, even three months old. That is unacceptable and easy to fix.

It wasn't that long ago that our systems had a difficult time pulling data and transforming it to a new format for use in a timely manner. But those days are gone, and technology has easily solved the problem. In many respects, this is where the traditional "big data" vendors can help your organization, by improving your data frequency.

Don't make this the reason why you can't make good decisions. Of all of the things that are obstacles to being a DDHO, how frequently you receive your data shouldn't be one of them. Invest in some moderately priced systems that support your data needs and the right resources to extract, transform, and load that data, and then we can move on to the business of why and to whom we will present the data.

WHY DO WE WANT TO VISUALLY REPRESENT OUR DATA?

Believe it or not, reading these words and translating them into something meaningful is a lot of work for your brain (Medina, 2008). A picture speaks volumes, so it's natural to assume that if we visualize data, we will convey more and better information.

> *Research shows that when numbers are properly framed, ordinary people are more capable of handling them than many medical professionals assume.*
>
> —Thomas Goetz

This is true regardless of who you are—doctor, patient, caregiver, or member of a health insurance plan. Being able to have access to your data and have that data presented in a way that helps you understand and make better decisions is a key role of data-driven healthcare. But just rushing to "dashboards" is not the right thing to do; not everyone who consumes information does so in the same way. It's important for each healthcare organization that strives to become a DDHO to consider that providing information to the user must be done with respect to that user's ability to consume it. In order to do this, you must first decide whom your information is going to be sent to and of those populations which ones take priority or have a higher allocation of resources. It's safe to assume that most provider organizations will find a way to ensure that physicians have access to clear, concise data quickly. Obviously our executive's information needs must be supported as well. Patients and members need to be considered during this time, in addition to your extended staff and management teams. Once you determine how many different groups your BI function will support, you will need to determine the allocation of effort for each of these groups. As tempting as it is to say that you will provide all information to all groups, that is not feasible. You may very well be able to deliver one set of reports that meet multiple groups needs, but there will be group-specific needs that will have to be managed.

Once your groups are identified and prioritized, you can take each group and determine if there are any subgroups that are important to address. A good example is your patient group. Within that group many may be considered elderly, not only making sending information to them challenging, but design considerations for aging eyes should be considered as well. The more tools you have in the toolbox, the better odds you will have of supporting your entire user base. A fascinating new product is available and may be worth considering for a certain part of your population; it's called Narrative Science.

Narrative Science was spun out of a team of students and professors at Northwestern University. Using a combination of statistics, computer science, and journalism, the team created an artificial intelligence platform now known as Quill™ (Narrative Science, 2014). Simply stated, Quill is software that analyzes data to extract meaning and insight and then presents that insight as a natural language report. More important, Quill focuses on explanations, not answers. In other words, it doesn't just say "You are at risk for diabetes"; it explains why. For a large part of your user base, this could be a very compelling way of understanding their information.

Someday spreadsheets will be as outdated as punch cards are today.

—Kris Hammond, chief scientist, Narrative Science

It flies in the face of the direction the industry is going today and has been going for a number of years now, but having the ability to presenting data in a textual way may very well be the only way that you can communicate with a good portion of your population. In addition, clinicians may be more comfortable presenting clinical data to patients if they have the ability to provide direction associated with the clinical content and how it's written. The best part is that it is all automated, so once you create the framework for the text, it is reused as appropriate. Imagine getting a lab report that reads more like the morning paper than the typical columnar-type report we get from our labs now. If it explained in plain English that your cholesterol is up and so is your weight, it's time to talk with your doctor. It's a compelling idea, and one that makes a lot of sense. As much as I like a good dashboard, not everyone can consume these types of reports. In many cases dashboards are poorly designed and don't communicate the important pieces of information, anyway. I don't think Narrative Science solves all of your problems, but I do think that it is onto something, and it could very well cure the issues associated with the older population and certain physician specialties.

Kris Hammond, chief scientist at Narrative Science, is clearly passionate about what this product is capable of doing and the future of BI. Narrative Science started out by reporting college baseball game recaps. "With the college baseball stats, the stories had to be compelling. If you read many of them, it was important to be consistent but not duplicative," says Hammond.

Utilizing variability, language choices, and picking words most evocative for the situation allows each Quill report to look and feel different, ensuring that the reader is as engaged as they can be in the social contract that is implied in reporting information, the introduction, explanation, and trading of ideas.

LEARNING A NEW LANGUAGE

For years I've felt that learning to understand data and the visualization of data was like learning a new language. It has a different alphabet, different grammatical rules, and, depending on who's developing that data, it can vary greatly. How do we go about learning a new language? First we listen and pay attention to those who already know it. Then we try to repeat what we've heard from something simple. We repeat and look for reassurance that we are on the right track. Then we branch out on our own, researching and reading, listening and repeating until we feel like we have a firm grip on the basics. That's exactly what's happening today, everywhere, from our Facebook posts and associated data to our work. Regardless of their role or background, people who have never thought about data before are trying to understand it, reconcile it, and make decisions from it.

I recently taught some classes for a local organization on how to use data to make better decisions. It was a very basic class, starting with the basics of what is important for them to know. Everyone's take on this is a little different, but I wanted them to understand how to read a population, so we talked about the measures of central tendency. Then I wanted them to apply that to popular media to see how easy it is to mislead people into either seeing or ignoring important aspects of the data. Then we spent a lot of time on the visualization of data and how easy it is to mislead people with data, even when you're not trying.

The goal of this course was to improve the base-level understanding of data, and to be a skeptical consumer in today's fire-hose data world. The class was geared toward managers and leaders of the organization and it was created because this particular company understood that their staff didn't have the skill set in many cases that was required to use data that is a standard part of our world today. They understood that they had to acquire a new language. They were right. They have a staff that is highly dedicated and bright, but had grown up in an industry that was less data driven than it is today. In order to get your organization ready to take on data and become data driven and action oriented you can't just assume that people intuitively understand data, even when it's visualized. Most people don't and they won't ask questions because they don't want to be considered stupid or ill-informed.

A MULTIMEDIA APPROACH TO CONSUMABLE DATA

Your data is no good just sitting around. It has to be presented to your user base. I always tell my clients that you have to begin with the end in mind when it comes to presenting your data. That means that you have to understand not only whom you're presenting it to but what they are going to do with to do so it. What decisions do people have to make from this data? Obviously a lot of different types of decisions can be made from the data that you are presenting. There's the regulatory aspect of the data; while it may seem like a checkbox activity, your organization will be judged on its effectiveness based on that data. So, long before you submit the regulatory reports to the appropriate groups, you should know and understand what those reports are going to say about your organization. You should also be prepared to make decisions that will alter the results of these reports. If your data reflects a lack of e-prescribing or electronic discharge instructions, then work on the processes that can improve those numbers long before you have to formally submit the report. Don't assume that those numbers are easily understandable for your internal audience, either. For some people in your organization, that will be the first time they will be seeing those pieces of information. Spend time preparing that data for consumption as well so you are not wasting resources because of bad data presentation.

Administrators and your executive physicians are a special group of end users. For many years the dashboard was the way to their desktop. I often say that for this group, your goal is to be as simple as possible, not because they can't understand the data—quite the opposite—but because they don't have time. But there are too many nuances to ignore for this group of end users. First, there are things that they just need to know: Is it going well? If the answer is yes, then it's fine to move on to something else. But if the answer is no, then they may need to dig in. Dashboards aren't always the right way to do that. This is highly dependent on the end user, and it's important that you understand your user base as well as possible to ensure that you deliver the right information to them in the right way.

The group that will be the most difficult to deliver for, because we've never really done it before, is our patients. I believe that in order for data and information to truly transform healthcare, we must provide better information to patients about their diagnosis, their treatment options, and their role in health. This data should be not only consumable but also easily available.

> *There is no established visual language for this diversity of data sources and consumption.*
>
> —Tomoko Ichikawa, senior lecturer of design at the Illinois Institute of Technology's Design School (Hardy, 2014)

Understanding your user base is important. Just as important is to understand that one way to present data is not the only way to present data. In other words, don't turn everything into a dashboard and call it a day. The data we are dealing with today is highly complex, and not all of it belongs in a graph, animated or otherwise. I know the latest trend is to make everything 3D and animated, but I'm here to tell you that most people will look at that and have no idea what that means. They won't say that to you, but just because you have presented the data in a way that is colorful and animated and looks cool doesn't mean it will help in comprehension, and that is the goal.

It's time to diversify your portfolio. Approach your information presentation layer as you would your retirement, and diversify. You will always need to visualize data (there's too much of it not to), but don't *merely* visualize it. Sometimes words are the only way that you can really get a point across or provide enough context on a highly complicated and sensitive topic, like an individual's health.

When you do visualize it, please keep it simple. I had a forensics (public speaking) coach in college who always repeated this mantra: "Keep it simple, stupid" (KISS). The real test of your ability to clearly explain a topic is how simple you can make it. Anyone can obfuscate a topic; it happens when you don't understand it that well. Anyone can take your data and make it jump off a screen (sometimes literally), but not just anyone can make it clearly represent the data. Much like that popular show *CSI*, let the data tell the story, not the software.

If at some point you find yourself surrounded by highly sophisticated analysts who want to take it to the next level, then by all means make that data leap. But for the most part your users have day jobs, and decoding complex visualizations shouldn't be one of them.

I disagree with a lot of the popular research on this topic. I don't think the average person, learning this new data language, can consume 18 colors. I don't think they can consume more than two axes, and I don't think they really want to. I believe people want their data shared with them in a way that highlights its important aspects and helps them take the next step in the health of their organization or their own body. If that takes a plain old bar chart or a paragraph of explanation, so be it. Meet them where they are.

REFERENCES

Goetz, T. (2010). "The Second Rule: Let Data Do the Work." In T. Goetz, *The Decision Tree: Taking Control of Your Health in the New Era of Personalized Medicine* (p. xvii). New York: Rodale.

Hardy, Q. (2014, January 7). "A Makeover for Maps." *New York Times*, p. B1.

Medina, J. (2008). *Brain Rules: 12 Principles for Surviving and Thriving at Work, Home and School*. Seattle: Pear Press.

Narrative Science. (2014, January). "Our Story." Retrieved March 10, 2014, from Narrative Science: http://narrativescience.com/company/our-story/.

Wikipedia. (2014, February 21). "Infographic." Retrieved March 10, 2014, from Wikipedia: http://en.wikipedia.org/wiki/Infographic.

CHAPTER 8

Data Privacy and Confidentiality: A Brave New World

Imagine that you walk into a nice restaurant, one that was recommended by someone you trust. You sit down and wait patiently as you get your water, bread, and order taken. Eventually you finish your meal, and you request the bill, handing over your credit card to expedite the process. The server comes back with your credit card and says simply, "We will get back to you." They've taken all of your information, and you will be notified of the amount at a later date. Imagine then that the servers, bartenders, dishwashers, perhaps even some of their suppliers discuss you at length. They discuss your preparedness to pay and perhaps even some psychological attributes about you. Eventually you get a bill after it's been reviewed by yet another entity, and you pay it with little knowledge of all of the places your data touched.

That's healthcare. Granted, our physicians are much better trained than your average waitstaff, but the premise is the same. They provide a service for you and about you, yet your access to the information about that service is owned by them. Doesn't that seem odd to you? Can you name one other industry where that's true?

There was a time when doctors didn't tell patients anything. You could have some horrible disease, on your deathbed, and they wouldn't tell you. That was true for me, and it wasn't that many years ago. I had been suffering, in pain, asking for help, and the doctors all just nodded and patted my head. Eventually I was referred to a specialist in the Twin Cities. I read my paper medical record and learned that my physician had written her suspected diagnosis nearly two years before that moment and never said a word to me about it. How is that okay?

In no other industry is your data so far out of your reach. Could you imagine if your bank did that? You'd leave faster than you could swipe your credit card, and probably report them. Did you know that it is a federal regulation that you can have access to your medical record? All of us could ask for it today, yet very few of us do. Is that why doctors keep things from us? Because they know we don't want to know? Or is it because we like to keep our heads down and our hopes high? Denial is a powerful thing.

Obviously keeping data confidential from people who shouldn't have access to it is something we are all interested in. But why keep information and data confidential from the person it's about? I believe it's a leftover from days when no one questioned doctors and people didn't want to know more; they just wanted to be fixed. There is still a lot of that thinking around today—give me a drug or a surgery, fix me mentally. That mentality is changing very fast, faster than many organizations can keep up. As the younger generation becomes of age and out from their parents' watchful eye they see their health data as just another piece of information, and they don't consider it as sacred or untouchable as generations before them.

WHO OWNS THE DATA?

Historically, healthcare organizations where you seek care have owned your data. The word *owned* is a provocative one in this instance and perhaps not all that relevant. Perhaps *stewardship* or *custodianship* are better terms to represent our accountability associated with data. Today, healthcare organizations are custodians of that data because they created it, but it's about you and it was created in the name of your care. But who *should* be the custodian *of* your data? This subject is at the crux of the privacy and confidentiality argument. As long as you don't steward your data, you are not really sure who has access to it, regardless of how many HIPAA statements you sign. I'm not sure any of us are prepared to own our own data, and for now it will reside in healthcare organizations, which means we, as healthcare organizations, have a responsibility to be good stewards of that data and be prepared to present it to patients in a manner that is useful to them.

Part of that responsibility means that we have to be sensitive to the changing tides of privacy and confidentiality. Today, there is much debate about what it means to have your data private and confidential. Those debates rage on because all too often we hear of data breaches that are preventable; it's hard not to be very critical about the organizations that are at the center of these breaches. At my organization, a services organization, we are very aware of the fact that our consultants touch very sensitive data every day. We have very clear rules about that, and we are trained annually on HIPAA regulations. But that doesn't mean something can't happen. Yes, laptops are encrypted, but often we don't shut off our machines (it's a hassle, since they take so long to boot because of the encryption software), so we just log off, which won't protect you. No question, some data breaches are a result of the uninformed or nonsensical. Leaving your laptop in plain sight while you frequent a bar is probably not advisable behavior.

When I started my career, I worked for a hospital that had contracted with a software company to make some proprietary software for use by our patients. We spent a lot of time thinking about the user interface. We considered how the patients would or could answer questions or attempt to avoid answering questions, and we designed the software to make it as difficult as possible for them to skip questions or answers in a way that didn't make sense. How often do we do that with our data? Are we as aggressive as we can be with our systems in the backend? Many gifted security officers are asking those questions every day, but they may not have the organizational support or budget to execute against those measures. We can do the checkbox activities to ensure that we are legally protected if a person leaves his laptop in the car while he goes out for Thirsty Thursday, but in the not-too-distant future, the checkbox activity for protecting data won't be enough. The demand for data is increasing, and that data needs to be available to patients through mobile devices. We will have to become very creative about how we protect privacy and confidentiality while allowing people to access data when they want and how they want. As described in *Nursing World*,

> Advances in technology, including computerized medical databases, the Internet, and telehealth, have opened the door to potential, unintentional breaches of private/confidential health information. Protection of privacy/confidentiality is essential to the trusting relationship between health care providers and patients. Quality patient care requires the communication of relevant information between health professionals and/or health systems. Nurses and other health professionals who regularly work with

patients and their confidential medical records should contribute to the development of standards, policies, and laws that protect patient privacy and the confidentiality of health records/information.

American Nurses Association, 2014

BARRIERS ARE EVERYWHERE

Protecting data sounds like a very simple thing to do. But it's about as difficult as a task can be. It's a lot like trying to prevent a flood where the water will go wherever it wants to go. In most cases we aren't sure where the data is, who has touched it, and when or why. It's not just a technology issue; it's a process issue. In the news last night I heard of a local health insurance company that was reporting a breach of information from nearly five years ago. The employee took home 38,000 records and asked a family member to reformat the file so the employee could work on it. That's clearly a preventable data breach. The employee should never have been allowed to take that data home, but let's just say this individual knew that and did it anyway. Why did this person need a family member to reformat the file? You can have the best technology in the world, but when the process is violated to such a degree, there's not much that technology can do.

Where do we begin? We are still responsible for this data, and while opinions are changing regarding privacy, we still have to deal with the issue that exists today. I'm no security expert, but I've done my fair share of process improvement projects. I know that it's rarely just one thing that happens that causes a data breach. It's a series of failures that lead to a breach.

- Lack of encryption (no excuse for lack of encryption)
- Not shutting off your machine (only way encryption actually works)
- Allowing people to save data to personal drives or thumb drives
- Giving consultants laptops

Many of these examples exist because we don't want to get in the way of people doing their jobs. We don't want to slow them down so we don't impose a shutdown policy. We want to take advantage of the consultant's time so we give her a laptop so she can work wherever. Any one of these things may not lead to a breach, but tack it onto a lack of insight or clarity on what the policy is and *why* it exists and you can see how breaches happen. Of course there is always that situation where someone purposefully hacks into your system to get data out. Technology can fix those scenarios if invested in appropriately.

PROCESS AND TECHNOLOGY

Start to reconsider your privacy practices in the context of your average employee. What are the top-10 scenarios in which your average employee could inadvertently be part of a data breach? Then create processes and procedures around those, with technology leading the way. If you turn the issue just slightly on its head, you might find a way to prevent the next data breach. What about the nurse or doctor who gets called out of the room and doesn't log off? Do you think that the machine will lock up? Maybe it doesn't—it happened to me just this week. The nurse left the room, didn't log off, and the machine didn't lock up. She came back 20 minutes later to the same screen she had up.

There are scenarios where the data itself is structured in a way that makes it a little too easy to inadvertently expose it. Part of this process is to do an annual review of your data-intensive applications, whether they create data, move data, or store data, and look for ways that the software or processes surrounding the software have been modified since the last review that could potentially lead to a data breach. There is no way that you can prevent every possible scenario; that's why annual reviews have to be an important part of your data security protocol.

No self-respecting healthcare organizations would call themselves data driven if they didn't have a robust process in place to appropriately protect the privacy and confidentiality of their patients' data. Put together a group of people who think about this problem differently, and, working with your security team, plan for ways to protect the data. Create a data classification document that outlines the different sensitivities of certain data and the procedures to follow to protect that data. Include that data classification document as part of your data governance effort. Annual reviews will also be a good time to take the temperature of the marketplace and determine if attitudes regarding privacy and confidentiality have changed enough to reconsider some policies. Start planning now for presenting data to patients in a new and compelling way. This has many more privacy and confidentiality concerns associated with it.

Frankly, there is no way to prevent these breaches. They will happen. If you're committing to be a data-driven organization, you have to recognize that it requires data and that presents some risks. You will have to become much more aware of how data is moved and managed throughout your organization now. This isn't just an IT issue; this is an organizational issue.

REFERENCE

American Nurses Association. (2014, March). "Privacy and Confidentiality." Retrieved March 22, 2014, from *Nursing World*: http://www.nursingworld .org/MainMenuCategories/Policy-Advocacy/Positions-and-Resolutions/ ANAPositionStatements/Position-Statements-Alphabetically/Privacyand- Confidentiality.html.

CHAPTER **9**

A Call to Action

Rapid change sweeps aside the status quo and those that defend it (the stuck former geniuses and the stuck bureaucrats). It replaces them with those willing to leap.

—Seth Godin

I n the preface of my first book, *Healthcare Business Intelligence,* I shared my personal story of how I became interested in healthcare. My journey through healthcare as a young patient helped me realize my career. Coincidentally, as I came to the end of this book, my healthcare journey that started more than 20 years ago took a sudden turn that required additional intervention. Frankly, it was a shock. I had thought that perhaps I was one of the lucky ones.

As I started down this path again, I was faced with many difficult choices. Of course, those choices are different now, being a 40-year-old versus a teenager. I also have a different perspective, a professional one, which makes me question and analyze all aspects of healthcare. It's easy to get lost in the details of this work and forget about the patient.

What would it mean to a patient, in this case me, if we became data driven? I suspect that in many cases a patient wouldn't notice too many differences. That's because most care is data driven. The surgical procedure that I had was based on years of research and honed to perfection to reduce errors and infection rates. The follow-up medication management is also based on decades of research, some of which I participated in 20 years ago. But you don't have to look much deeper to see other data-driven opportunities. The ability to improve how our organizations are run could save countless dollars. Those dollars could be put back into other areas of research or improvements, or reduce the overall spending on healthcare that leads directly to our patients' pocketbooks.

Of course, there's the ubiquitous "If we had the data, we could research every disease state and improve care," and no doubt that is true. So, if we know that the data could help save money and improve care, what are we waiting for?

Hopefully the preceding pages have brought you to the end willing and able to take on what you need to do to become a data-driven healthcare organization. Operationalizing the theoretical is important in this instance; we have to be able to take what we learned from these pages and implement it. We can take a page or two from business process management as we attempt to make these changes. After all, much of what we are doing is optimizing processes. But it's not all that we are doing, and there has to be a heavy dose of agile methods, evaluation, and healthcare knowledge in the mix, too. That's why I originally proposed RISE (reduce, identify, streamline, evaluate), simply as a framework to ensure that your organization can take the multifaceted approach to change management. The keyword is "simply." This is complex enough; we don't need to introduce more complexity into it.

The first year on your data-driven healthcare organization (DDHO) journey will be full of bumps and bruises, but remember, the end justifies the means. One of my favorite lines to new clients is "The only thing I can promise you is that something will go wrong. What matters is how we respond to it." Healthcare organizations have taken on so much change in the last five years. You know how to do that; what we will focus on now is how to frame this effort and what to do when something goes wrong, because it will.

First and foremost, you have to ensure that your organization is ready. In my first book, I included a survey that assesses your organization's readiness for change. I've included it in Appendix A for your reference. It's your first stop on the data-driven journey. The truth is, if your organization isn't ready for what's in front of it, don't bother. That doesn't mean you can just avoid the work; there are things you can do in the interim to prepare your organization. It just means you aren't yet ready for your DDHO journey.

If you passed that hurdle, you next have to assess your leader. Who's going to run with this? It doesn't have to be a full-time position with a corresponding title; it just has to be someone who can rally the troops and demonstrate some management discipline. If you have a committee that's ready to take it on, that's okay, too, but committees have a hard time making day-to-day decisions. Remember, a key attribute of a DDHO is *action*.

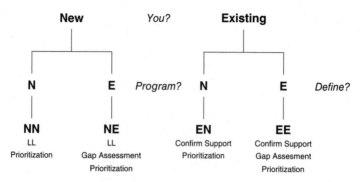

Figure 9.1 NN-NE-EN-EE

It's important to ensure that whoever is going to run with it has the full support of the leadership of the organization. That means the willingness to remove obstacles and to sign checks. Those two are introductory obstacles that, if you're serious, shouldn't take more than a week or two to complete.

It occurred to me as I was working on this chapter that not all situations are created equal. For instance, one of the first things I do when I am introduced to a new client is to determine how long the leader has been there and whether there is an established program. The answers to the questions will determine the approach that needs to be taken. Many efforts will be transferable regardless of whether you are new or the program is new. But in some cases there will be a few extra steps along the way. (See Figure 9.1.)

It's important to mention that regulatory reporting is different from what we are working on here. Those requirements are not mandated by you; therefore, they should be managed as a separate group. It makes sense organizationally to have that function report up through the business intelligence (BI) leader since he or she will be using the same data.

APPLYING RISE TO YOUR EFFORTS

Odds are you know how to get a project completed in your organization. Whatever method you use (agile, waterfall, etc.), I don't need to tell you how to execute projects. Admittedly, data warehousing and BI are slightly different animals than the average IT project. Add the complexities of healthcare on top of that and you have the fixings for some potentially challenging days ahead. The RISE framework should help alleviate some of the challenges. Here again are the four cornerstones of closing the innovation gap in healthcare:

1. Reduce the unknowns.
2. Identify the alternatives.
3. Streamline the standards.
4. Evaluate the effort.

The advantage of RISE is that it can be applied regardless of how you do projects or where you are in your project life cycle. It's a complementary framework that helps keep you grounded in the work.

SOME DISTINCTIONS ABOUT BEING NEW

Congratulations! You have a new job and an incredible opportunity to create a program that will help your new organization become data driven. It's an exciting time for you. Once the honeymoon wears off, though, you may start to feel nervous about the task in front of you. Let's break it down and take it one step at a time.

First, spend some time getting the lay of the land. That's important for any new job. You don't want to be a bulldozer coming

► GET THE LAY OF THE LAND

Asking a lot of questions early on will help you understand the work that's ahead of you. It's helpful to know: What's already there? Who uses it? How do they use it? What decisions are made from it? What are the pain points? Who are the biggest cheerleaders? Who are the biggest detractors? Why are they not supportive? What is the technology platform? How much does it cost to maintain? What are the architectural considerations? What are the standards that have been adopted? Are there any architectural guidelines? Is the organization willing to be an early adopter?

Not new to the organization? Maybe it doesn't matter. We have to ask ourselves some really difficult questions, and the answer can't be "That's how we've always done it." If you've been around awhile, it might be time to get the lay of the land again.

in and making changes without context. When I start with a new client, I always take the time to understand their specific organization and their wants and needs. Granted, there are a lot of similarities, but where there are differences is where real change can happen.

GETTING STARTED

I'm a fan of *joint application design (JAD)* sessions. They're commonly used to create requirements for projects. JAD accelerates the effort because you get all the key people in a room and you formally move through the different levels of requirements until you have something you can build. It is particularly effective when you have a large project or a project that isn't well known (or supported). In this case, I believe the format for a JAD is appropriate, but we aren't building requirements per se, more like creating requirements for the program. Regardless of what you call it, the method and discipline of JADs is what's important.

Our JAD will walk through the RISE framework in order to get a broad-based understanding of what the organization wants. The assumption is that your organization wants to become data driven, but the mechanisms to do that can vary by organization. The JAD serves a secondary purpose, too; it's a method of communication to the organization that this is starting.

The participants in the JAD session are critical to the success of the effort. You will need to invite the key stakeholders, those people who have the most to gain (or lose), the BI leaders, your cheerleaders and detractors. You will want to assign a formal record keeper for the session as well.

The agenda for the JAD will include:

- The goal of the program.
- The objectives of the program.
- What's unknown or risky?
- Standardization:

- Current state?
- Any changes on the horizon?
- Evaluation criteria:
  - Identify how you want to measure the program (make it as objective/measurable as possible).
  - Determine the timing of the evaluations, which will serve as a stage gate for the program.
- Action items.

▶ A SAMPLE AGENDA IS AVAILABLE IN APPENDIX E

It's important to facilitate this session so that it doesn't go off the rails. Each of these topics could take days if you let them. You need to time-box each topic to ensure that you will have time to get through everything. The JAD will likely take a full day, perhaps even a day and a half. That sounds like a lot of time, especially with the guest list, but it's a small price to pay to know the parameters of the goals and the success factors. Knowing these things will give you the room to do your job and save time in the long run.

Some discussion points for the session: Discuss the program as an entity, what you want to see as part of that, including organizational implications. Review the five tenets of healthcare business intelligence (Appendix B): data quality, value, technology and architecture, leadership and sponsorship, and cultural/organizational implications. When discussing the unknowns or risks, keep that dialogue open; nothing should be off the table. But as people bring content up, they should be willing to identify the alternatives to those unknowns and risks. That should include people, process, and technology. Now is the time to identify pilots or proofs of concepts that can help manage the most risky propositions.

When the session is complete, you will need to review the documentation with your team. Make sure that everyone understands what was discussed and the next steps. Your team is the one that will operationalize this effort, so they should be comfortable.

After the JAD session, you will have a lot of work projects identified. It's important to know how they will impact your staffing and timelines. If you don't have a quick method to do that, check out the table in Appendix C: Assessing Available Time.

YOU KNOW WHAT THEY SAY ABOUT ASSUMING

We outlined some distinctions about being new. Now it's time to consider those situations where you've been around for a while. Being an existing employee who is taking on BI often means lots of advantages, but it's important that you don't get too complacent. If you think that a JAD session would be helpful to you, then by all means do one. A few years ago I had a client ask me if I could help him with some facilitated JAD sessions. He was new to his role, and one of the departments, located in another state, was throwing up some major obstacles to his efforts. After digging for the answer, he found that they had been doing things the way they wanted to for years because no one asked them if they needed help. It was easy for him to ask questions; he was new. The JAD session elicited requirements that his team was able to execute against. A day and a half of effort meant big wins for him and the department.

If you've been at your job for a while, it's hard to be objective. That's not always a bad thing. That experience and expertise can often be an advantage to understanding data or the operational procedures that get us data. But if you're not sure, perhaps there's that little voice in the back of your head saying "What if?" then take a step back and get the lay of the land.

WHAT DOES DATA MEAN TO YOU?

I've counseled you in these pages to plan, take your time, and determine if you are really ready. Of course, many of us don't feel that we have the luxury of doing most of that. There's pressure to just start building and figure out what you're building later. I certainly understand that pressure and the need to find a balance between planning and being thorough.

In the first chapter I recommended a SWOT (strengths, weaknesses, opportunities, threats) analysis. I believe that this is a good way to assess the value of the program. It allows you to look outside your own organization into the broader marketplace, which is a significant consideration right now.

TRANSFORMING AN INDUSTRY

You can almost *hear* the transformation. Mergers and acquisitions, an entire new industry created to help analyze healthcare data—it is change on a massive scale. Using this data to help your organization seems to make sense, considering the value that is lying there.

Just thinking about a problem in a new way is helpful. There are a million business models and frameworks out there that are meant to help organizations bring order out of chaos. My modest attempt at a framework, RISE, was created to help healthcare organizations close the innovation gap. There are aspects of the RISE framework that are a lot like others, but including managing the risk with streamlining standards means RISE is a different way of thinking than most other frameworks.

Think of RISE as something that you can go back to. It's not something that will dictate how you do a project; there are much better methods to do that. But it will help you pick up the pace while managing risk and adapting standards, because it's not the change that's the issue (necessarily), it's the pace of the change that has been a challenge for most organizations. It seems that as soon as you get a good handle on what you are working on, the requirements or strategies change, and some of those changes are outside your control. Most data projects have a natural pace to them that's very different from what is expected today.

Writing a book is actually quite similar. There have been many times in this process that I've gotten lost in the detail. I've had to remind myself of the point of this effort; you will probably have to do that, too.

> *Data-driven means that information must be consumable, and contextual, to encourage action that will modify behavior over time.*

DATA STANDARDIZATION

One of the biggest challenges facing healthcare today is data standardization. We have plenty of standards—we are getting closer to the Holy Grail—but there are still the "Towers of Babel" that impede progress.

Not only do we have challenges with standard consistency; we also have the clinical concepts. When I was working on my master's degree, we spent a lot of time understanding the impact of slight variations in data creation and acquisition. Most statisticians will tell you that it is one of the most difficult things to manage for, because it's beyond the control of the statistical methods you apply to it. Any good clinical trial goes into an extraordinary amount of detail to ensure that there is a lot of consistency to allow us to compare results. We lose that rigor in a typical clinical setting.

Finally, there is the provocative topic of a truly unique patient ID. I cannot solve for the political challenges that are associated with this issue. What I do know is that many of the data challenges could be solved with a unique patient ID. Until then, many organizations have adapted master patient indexes, and that may have to suffice.

THE NEXT STEP IN BI MATURITY

The biggest way that we can advance the maturity of our BI programs is to close the innovation gap. The good news is that there are so many disruptive technologies available to us that we should be able to find what meets our needs. I defined disruptive technologies in Chapter 4 as needing to:

- Integrate structured, unstructured, and semi-structured data from many disparate systems.
- Do it very quickly.
- Provide a stable environment that supports sophisticated security requirements.
- Be cost effective.
- Provide contextual data in a highly consumable format to encourage self-service.

After looking at many options, I believe the *modern data platform* offers us many of the disruptive technologies that we need to accelerate our data warehouse and BI maturity. It is the new way forward.

CREATING THE DDHO

In my first book. I outlined the five tenets of healthcare BI. The first few months I was working on that book, I only had four tenets, then I came to the realization that cultural implications were a major tenet and needed to be addressed. Your ability to create a true DDHO is highly contingent on the cultural change that will or will not occur in your organization. In Chapter 5 of this book, I outlined four things that are critical to getting your organization started, and they vary slightly from creating just a BI program to creating a DDHO. The organizational structure of the BI team is important to the success of the DDHO. I'm not saying that you *have* to hire a chief data officer who reports up to a line of business, but the closer the data and BI programs are aligned with business, the better off you are. If you can achieve that with a highly actualized chief information officer, then by all means do so. The other implication for the organization is the actual structure. The idea of a hub-and-spoke model allows you to centralize standards of best practices while leaving data and operational expertise in each independent department. The risk you run if you don't do that is that your team gets so large it's difficult to manage (and may require a leader at the executive level).

Follow these four steps to create the DDHO:

1. Change the organizational structure.
2. Train business users to become more savvy data consumers.
3. Readjust data governance to align with a modern data platform.
4. Adopt a modern data platform.

"BIG DATA"

I would be thrilled if I never had to utter the term *"big data"* again. In Chapter 6, I redefine *"big data"* to what is impactful to healthcare, that is, *diverse and persistent data (DPD)*. Diverse, persistent data is the future of healthcare, and the good news is that there are products and vendors that are available to support our brave new world. The question is, how do we use them, and when? Not all DPD is created equal, and that's true for the corresponding vendors.

I love the approach that Premier takes, as outlined in Chapter 6. It's a traditional coordinated effort using proofs of concept and pilot projects. We should all take a page from their book. They found value in many of these systems, and they have much more data than the average provider organization.

I still want you to tread carefully. I don't believe the "big data" industry has matured yet. Until that pendulum swings the other way, there are a lot of vendors and service providers out there that may not be there in a year or two.

MAKE YOUR DATA CONSUMABLE

One of the key attributes of being a DDHO is that all the work is based on action. You have the ability to use data to make better, faster decisions. In addition, you have to educate your end users to improve their ability to consume data. One major step to achieve both of those goals is to really think about how you present your data. So often we think about that as the very last step. We are getting better overall, because many of the available software packages have much better visualization capability. But just because you *can* do a 3D pie graph doesn't mean you should. There is so much data available to you and your end users that we are all at risk of information overload. It's critical now, more than ever, that we ensure that everything we present tells a story and answers the question "So what?"

I rarely talk about specific products, but one that I find very intriguing in the context of making your data more consumable is Narrative Science. I think that it addresses many of the issues we have with visualizing data, particularly clinical data. Physicians are notoriously cautious about talking about certain clinical data with patients, because patients have a tendency to not fully understand the implications. Word choice is critical when explaining challenging clinical concepts, even in terms of cholesterol (remember when *good* was just good and *bad* was bad?).

Therefore, it's not just about making data visual—it's about making it consumable. If you're able to do that, you are well on your way to being a DDHO.

PRIVACY AND CONFIDENTIALITY

This is perhaps one of the most dynamic and changing topics, which is saying something considering the current status of both data warehousing and "big data." I predict a major shift in privacy and confidentiality over the next 5 to 10 years. That will have major implications for our work. The trouble is that it isn't happening yet, and we are still responsible for keeping that data secure.

FINAL THOUGHTS ON DATA-DRIVEN HEALTHCARE

It wasn't part of the plan to have a healthcare crisis during the writing of this book. The fact that it was the same healthcare crisis I had 20 years ago that forced me into healthcare data is not lost on me. When I started, we were still delivering reports on paper via interoffice memo. That was only 15 years ago; it's really amazing what has changed in that short amount of time. I am thrilled to be part of this industry. Despite the changes and the challenges, to be on the forefront at a time when the industry is going through a revolution is an honor.

The hard work is in front of us. The industry still has a lot of maturing to do. But data can change everything; it has changed everything, and it will do it again. It is our job now to help guide that change in the most innovative and responsible way possible.

APPENDIX **A**

Readiness for Change

HEALTHCARE BI MATURITY

	Yes	No	In Progress
Data Quality			
Do you have agreed-upon definitions for your data?			
Do you manage metadata?			
Do you have a data governance function operating?			
Do users trust the data?			
Leadership and Sponsorship			
Do you have an assigned BI Leader?			
Is the leader well respected throughout the organization?			
Do you have more than one sponsor?			
Do you have grassroots support?			
Technology and Architecture			
Do you currently follow ETL best practices?			
Do you have a data model?			
Is your hardware right-sized for performance and scalability?			
Do you have a trusted IT leader?			
Value			
Does the organization perceive BI as a value today?			
Do you have good user adoption?			
Do users feel that BI is critical to their ability to do their job?			
Does your BI function report up through the business?			
Assessing Readiness			
Has your organization made successful enterprise-wide changes in the past?			
Does your organization believe data can help make better decisions?			
Is your organization committed to data management?			
Is your organization prepared to make the changes necessary to adopt BI?			

To complete the questionnaire, have the BI leader and the executive sponsor take the time to complete it together. There will likely be some conversation but they should agree on the final answer. For each *Yes* you marked, give yourself two points, for each *No* you marked, give yourself zero points, and for each *In Progress* you marked, give yourself one point. Truthfulness is important for this assessment to work. Many of these questions are difficult to answer; questions about whether a leader is well respected, or even whether the hardware is right-sized, can open old wounds. It's essential that everyone understands that doing this assessment isn't about placing blame but about moving forward to deliver a great product to end users.

Maturity Stages

Your Score	Your Stage
0–10	Stage 1
11–30	Stage 2
31–40	Stage 3

Tenets of
Healthcare BI

Adapted from Laura Madsen, *Healthcare Business Intelligence: A Guide to Empowering Successful Data Reporting and Analytics* (Hoboken, NJ: John Wiley & Sons). Copyright ©2012.

THE FIVE TENETS

1. **Data quality:** It could be said that data quality is important to any industry, but it is absolutely critical to healthcare business intelligence (BI)—no one dies if a retail report misrepresents inventory in an end cap—so it lands in our number-one spot as the first tenet of healthcare BI. Perhaps more than any other tenet, quality data helps drive trust and user adoption of the program. Data quality is relative, and having high-quality data doesn't mean that your data is 100 percent accurate, because, after all, what is accurate? There are many aspects of data quality, including the concepts of data governance, data profiling, and data certification.

2. **Leadership and sponsorship:** Some of the most successful healthcare BI programs started because one person was absolutely passionate about the difference data can make to an organization. Long-term sponsorship requires full engagement and a knowledgeable staff. It means that the organization isn't just giving some time to it but is dedicating, fueling, and insisting that data becomes the lifeblood of the organization. It is a leadership activity, but doesn't always require a person in a traditional leadership role in your organization. We review the different levels of sponsorship and what it takes to support your sponsor for the long term.

3. **Technology and architecture:** To be clear, BI is not an information technology (IT) activity. But investing in the best practices associated with data modeling, extract, transform, and load (ETL), and solid BI applications will ensure performance and scalability. Data modeling doesn't get much more complicated than in healthcare. Ensuring the right data model will allow your program to flourish without having to change the tire at 60 miles per hour. Few industries have the fragmented and messy data that healthcare does. Healthcare data is fragmented, coming from many different systems

(electronic health records [EHRs], financial systems, etc.) and more often than not the data is driven from contextual information or data such as nurse notes. As a reference to our first tenet, ETL is the only way to make data usable to the average end user. We must ensure that the baseline IT-specific activities are addressed to allow time to focus on much of the other work in BI.

4. **Value:** Every aspect of healthcare BI must provide value. Healthcare organizations are overburdened and understaffed, particularly when it comes to data. There is no room for theoretical exercises or interesting investigations (that comes after you are well established). To get started, you must focus where BI can provide the organization with the most value. Much of what we discuss from a value perspective concerns the delivery of reports, dashboards, and ad-hoc analysis. We address how to best bring your business users with you, such as training and providing support. Finally, we evaluate your user base and determine how to best deliver value to each group.

5. **Cultural change:** Collaboration is the glue that holds a good BI team together. Ask any BI professional and you'll hear that much of the challenge isn't bad data quality or poor tools, but politics and organizational dynamics. I have worked with enough hospitals to tell you that our healthcare organizations are as susceptible to the pitfalls of human nature as any other organizations; some may even be worse than average. I was once told by a research assistant that I had a diplomatic way of solving issues. You will need as much diplomacy as a UN ambassador as you start this journey. You will encounter naysayers, me-too-ers, a glut of I-don't-have-the-time folks, and just-give-me-the-data responses. I have been in meetings with physicians, nurses, administrators, and finance gurus, and I have heard it all. You'll need the courage to stay above it all and continue to support a collaborative approach among all the stakeholders.

Bringing these five tenets together creates a fully functioning BI program that's optimized for success in a healthcare organization.

DATA QUALITY

Data quality by itself could be the subject of a long book. The importance of data quality really can't be underestimated in healthcare. It not only drives our ability to make decisions based on data, but it drives end-user adoption of BI programs. Few things kill BI programs faster than bad data.

It is important to recognize that there is no such thing as 100 percent clean data. That statement will disturb a few of you. I know this because when I make this statement in presentations throughout the country, one person in the audience makes an audible gasp. This statement is meant to be provocative, but it's also reality. Data is flawed from creation, and our ability to change that would require herculean efforts. But just because we don't seek out 100 percent clean data doesn't mean we cannot strive for a fully validated and certified data set. To do our work well, we must strive for the best data possible.

A number of years ago, I was working with a health plan to implement a BI product. I had acquired this customer from a previous product manager and had been at the implementation for more than two years. Most of our clients implemented in six to nine months, so I wondered, "Why is it taking so long?" The answer was data quality. They decided that 100 percent data quality was their goal, and two years later they were still working on data quality questions on every cell of a 10-plus-million-row database. A large team of analysts and businesspeople did the data profiling and then tracked down every errant entry. Once investigated, many of those errant entries resulted in a process change to the organization. The effort was admirable but flawed. The final cost of the project was staggering, and just a few weeks after going live its data was no longer 100 percent accurate.

The idea of tackling data quality seems overwhelming to many. Data comes in torrents every day, week, or month, depending on how often you bring it over. Determining what represents high-quality data in your organization and then deciding what to do about it can be a BI manager's worst nightmare. The good news is that's where data governance comes in. Data quality and data governance are forever entwined. Data governance is a process more than a product. It requires that business users of the data become owners of the data and take ownership over the data to define it, and then manage it within those parameters. The only real way to assess whether you have high-quality data is to have a data governance function that will tell you what *high quality* means.

Data governance administration is not the glamorous part of data quality (assuming there is a glamorous part), but it's important to ensure that you have a method to keep the data governance function running as smoothly as possible. Data governance administration entails the creation and management of the content created by the data stewards as well as by the data governance committees. Data stewards are the guardians of good-quality data in your organization.

To some organizations, high-quality data means nothing more than pulling data from the source systems and plopping it down—what some data warehouse consultants refer to as "suck and plunk." For others, it's nothing less than ensuring that the data is 100 percent clean. When I work with clients who are just getting started, I always recommend that they start with a data governance council and one question: How much data quality is good-enough data quality? Not all of the data is there for clinical decisions. Not all of the data is there for financial decisions. First determine the threshold for quality and then modify the BI processes to meet that threshold.

We have addressed the data quality once the data lands in the data warehouse (as part of the ETL process), but what about the data quality that comes directly out of the transactional systems, where our data lives? Data profiling, the method of analyzing data against parameters to determine if it fits the accepted profile, can be an incredibly powerful tool in your fight for high-quality data. Even if you have a team of analysts that knows your data like the back of its hand, data profiling quantifies all of the issues and helps the team know where the worst trouble spots are. When I was working on my master's degree, my first step was always data profiling, although I didn't call it that. My degree program trained me how to use data that already existed, but that meant I had to know what I was dealing with, warts and all. To do that, I would run frequencies on the data. Doing this provided me with the mean, median, mode, minimum, and maximum for each field of data. This type of base-level understanding of data helps an organization to identify data that is inherently inaccurate, but, more important, it shows where you can apply the business rules to ensure that the data that lands in your data warehouse is ready for use.

It might be important at this point to make a statement about usage. If your intention is to hire a whole bunch of really smart data analysts, then a data warehouse and BI program is not the most cost-effective method of getting the analysts the data they need to do their job. Data warehouses are created to ensure a broader user base. If you don't intend on investing in data quality for a warehouse to provide a broader user base with the data that they can use, then there's no reason to create a warehouse—a team of analysts can work just fine. However, keep in mind that data warehouse and BI programs are built for scalability and usage; a team of analysts is not. What works today with five data analysts may not function efficiently two years from now when data volumes have grown three times. In addition, if you are not applying a broadly accepted set of definitions to the data (such as business rules to define "bed days"), then each of your analysts is probably coming up with his or her own. That means that you will be sitting around the boardroom with three different answers to the same question.

Data profiling allows you to understand your data in a different way. Running the descriptive statistics (i.e., mean, median, mode) is helpful to assess the mess so you can apply the business rules in the warehouse. If you have no intention of fixing the data, then it's best that you don't allow the average end user access to the warehouse. Allowing access to a larger user base implies that your organization is looking to put data in end users' hands to broaden the ability of people throughout your organization to make better decisions.

Metadata Management

Other aspects of data management drive data quality, or perhaps the perception of data quality. Metadata management is closely related to data governance in that the decisions and actions of the data governance function must be played out in the metadata. But before I get too far into the idiosyncrasies of metadata, I have to answer an important question: What is *metadata*? The most popular definition is *data about data*. To me, that definition is less than useful. The analogy that best suits *metadata* is card catalogs and the Dewey Decimal System. Long before we used computers to find and read books, you would go directly to the card catalog to look up your book choice. The system included a method of looking up books by author's name. You simply went alphabetically until you found it. Then it would include a code, something like 123.11, designating a category and location. Then you would write that down and go find your book. A modern example of this type of simple metadata is how Ikea stores and distributes its furniture. There again, you write down a code and use it to find the location of the chair you want.

The best way to consider metadata is to understand how data is created, stored, and defined. There are actually three types of metadata. *Structural* metadata, which is the data about how the content is created, is not really about data at all since the data doesn't exist yet. For the purposes of BI, this type of metadata isn't really useful, but it does exist in the originating application (i.e., your EHR). *Technical* metadata is the data about where the content exists. In our case, that is the data warehouse. This technical metadata includes things like table name and column. At this point, this metadata is reported as ENCOUNTER_TBL.ENCOUNTER_ID, and it can go on for quite a while if you have a complicated data model. As the average end user would have no idea what this means, we have created business metadata. *Business* metadata includes all the data that applies to how end users want to see or understand the data. For example, if we are calculating our average length of stay (ALOS), we include the definition of ALOS: total number of patient days divided by the number of admissions and discharges over a specified time period. Then we include the impacted tables, such as UNIQUE_PT, ADMISSION_CNT & DISCHARGE_CNT, and finally the timetables (such as day, week, and month of year). Business metadata is the most important aspect of metadata because it helps end users understand how data is defined and calculated.

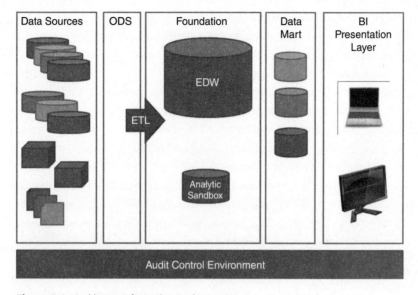

Figure B.1 Healthcare Information Environment

Now that we understand what metadata is, we can discuss how to manage it. Management of metadata is important because it allows end users exposure to the common definitions of the data. To do that, you must assign someone responsibility for taking what is decided by the data governance function and finalizing it into the metadata repository. Sometimes that's just a really big spreadsheet, and other times it's a separate software system or part of your BI Presentation Layer. Regardless of how you tackle the software aspect of metadata, it's important that you ensure that the process aspect of metadata is well documented and understood. But most important, you must provide business metadata to your end users so they understand the data they are using (see Figure B.1).

LEADERSHIP AND SPONSORSHIP

As an employee in a large corporation, it's easy to recognize the value of sponsorship. Frankly, few large-scale efforts get done in a corporation unless someone in a suit with a door is backing up your project.

You need this backing to gain momentum and legitimacy. That's the positive side of sponsorship. The negative side is about protecting yourself. One of my bosses explained to me once, "CYA, Laura. If it goes south, it's on them and not you. That's the only way you can survive." That boss shall remain nameless, for obvious reasons.

Let me tell you about a time when lack of sponsorship really took its toll. On a cold January day, the first week back from the holiday-haze, we received a call at the office. The request was simple: Did we have anyone who could come in and do a BI product assessment? The client had two BI products and wanted—needed—to consolidate. I was in the client's office the next day. On the surface, the request was so easy I could have probably done it in a few hours, but then she closed the door and told me the rest of the story.

Three years prior to this meeting, my client was in an enviable position. The organization had a fully integrated, well-modeled, and highly popular data warehouse. The manager (at the time) didn't feel like he needed a high degree of sponsorship because he had been incredibly successful without one. He never took the time to educate the leadership on the value of the team, the role it played in the organization, or the complexities associated with the work. As the organization grew, the business decided it was time for a new and updated financial system. Without even a nod to BI, they purchased (lock, stock, and barrel) a fully integrated application stack that included a black-box (supposedly industry-specific) data model, front-end tool, and packaged ETL scripts. The BI manager attempted to tell them the error of their ways to no avail. He left nine months later, exhausted from the fight.

As I sat in the office of the person now responsible for the deployment, she recognized where it had all fallen apart. She conceded that the lock, stock, and barrel product, while perhaps good in other settings, didn't fit their business and had failed miserably. The supposed "product consolidation" was really more of an effort to bring competing groups together for the common good, including a newly promoted VP who was now their executive sponsor.

What this client lacked was a sponsor who understood the ramifications of the decision. Good sponsorship is not a checkbox activity. It takes work to identify the right person, convince him or her of the importance, and then educate him or her on the key aspects of BI and data warehousing. There are three levels of sponsorship: *traditional, influencer,* and *grassroots.* Each of these levels can have a different perspective on sponsoring the program. Only the traditional and influencer levels have the potential to budget for the activity, but they also have the most to lose without it. The grassroots efforts feel the pain of the lack of cohesion every day; their support helps clarify the value to someone who can support the initiative financially. This is why leadership and sponsorship are different; you need people who understand the value and are willing to put their money where their mouth is.

The traditional executive sponsor is the one with the "right" title and the checkbook. Generally speaking, these are the C-level executives and vice presidents of the organization. But the challenge is that they have a million things on their plate, and it's hard for you to be heard above the fray. So when you walk into their office, they have not spent any time thinking about your project. To prepare for the possible directions the conversation may take, you will need to have a fair amount of back-pocket content, such as examples of possible dashboards, anecdotes from other organizations that have been successful, or even an action plan to get going. Keep in mind that they often have to deal with every aspect of managing an organization and you should try to predict their concerns and questions. Any time you go in front of an executive, you need to do your research. Spend some time getting to know the organization in a way you hadn't considered before. Talk with department heads of the organization and work to understand their daily needs and struggles. You will look like a rock-star supernova if you are ready with anything the executive fires at you.

As you are talking with the department heads, keep in mind that you are never really done looking for a sponsor. The other type of sponsor is the influencer; this person generally has a leadership title and is well respected among the senior leadership. The influencer is often the voice of reason that many leaders will listen to. The influencer can be your main connection to the executive sponsor. Keep in mind that the arguments to win over the influencer are different from the arguments to win over the executive. The influencers are looking for the projects that will make them even more indispensable in the eyes of the leadership or, even better, make them seem like prophets.

Finally, you have the grassroots effort. Although not technically a sponsor, the grassroots buildup of the project and program will be a short-term loss but a long-term gain. This grassroots effort is exactly what it sounds like; you build up enthusiasm and interest in the average end user. They become your cheerleaders and start to ask their bosses about the project and when things will get started. They'll begin telling other people, and eventually it will come around back to you when someone asks you about "this new BI thing." Then, and only then, do you know that your grassroots efforts will be successful.

Sponsorship ensures success. If you have addressed all three of these areas of sponsorship, even if you move on to bigger and better projects, the program will continue because a team of people is responsible for the leadership of the program.

BI programs are highly political. BI is like the UN of your organization. It brings everyone together for shared decision making and responsibility. Sometimes that means good things, like using data to better determine process improvement efforts for Lean Six Sigma. Other times it has to make really tough decisions about vendors or, worse, employees. Some people will be on your side and other people won't (maybe because they didn't think of it first). Good sponsorship across these three dimensions means that you are not alone fighting the good fight.

The support of these key stakeholders is critical to the long-term success of the function. At the end of the day, they hold the purse strings. One of the most consequential things you can do to gain executive support is to clearly articulate a vision and a return on investment (ROI). Several topics are controversial in the BI industry, and ROI is one of them. Many BI professionals will tell you that you can't get to an ROI because many of the benefits are soft and immeasurable. A "hard" ROI is a challenge in BI, but that doesn't mean we can dismiss it. We owe it to our leadership to put our money where our mouth is. If you can't do that, the likelihood of your BI function flourishing is highly unlikely.

One of the major drivers of ROI is end-user adoption. If users aren't adopting, then you won't be able to attribute better and faster decision making to your BI work. Creating a thorough and frequently delivered training program and support function will keep your users humming along. But if your data lacks the quality that users expect, this will challenge your success.

Communication is an important part of the BI program and falls under sponsorship. Ensuring that good information gets out to the entire organization can certainly drive value, but it really serves to reassure your sponsors that activities are getting done. To do this, I recommend a marketing plan. Marketing plans help you plan all of the activities associated with promoting what your team is doing to deliver value to the organization. Sometimes it can feel like a full-time job just communicating to end users, so having a good method of scheduling and documenting each communication can help a great deal.

TECHNOLOGY AND ARCHITECTURE

Memory is a funny thing. Research on the topic of memory and recall has shown that emotional experiences are permanently etched into our brain. Many of my stories here were part of the run-of-the-mill BI work I have done over the past decade. Healthcare BI work isn't the most emotional work; much of it is just questions about indexing and data quality. But sometimes the phone rings in the middle of the night, like it did back in 2001. I had been working for a payer organization that had grown by acquisition. The area I worked in was in charge of a new line of services we provided to pharmaceutical companies. The service provided phone-based nursing services to individuals taking an adherence-challenged medication. It was one of those medications where the cure was worse than the disease. It had the ability to do things like change the color of your irises. Our job was to deliver disease-management-type services as well as be on the other end to document adverse events.

To be clear, this wasn't part of our normal business model. In fact, it was just one of many changes that had occurred to the team over the previous 12 months. Many on the team had requested that we slow down and take the time to assess how the data was being collected and stored, but time wasn't on our side. Then the call came in at 11:00 P.M. on a Tuesday. The analyst simply said that she missed a join (a relationship in the data specific to how you write a query). It seemed like an innocuous thing to miss, but when you are responsible for reporting adverse events to the Food and Drug Administration (FDA), it is anything but innocuous.

That join meant that we missed reporting more than 10 documented adverse events to the FDA. That's a significant number when the total population taking this drug is only in the low thousands. The following weeks were filled with meetings with lawyers and marking all documentation with "Privileged and Confidential." We were investigated by the FDA, the client threatened a multimillion-dollar lawsuit, and the pharmaceutical services we provided were shuttered within months. Finally, the postmortem analysis of the disaster revealed what most of us on the team had known within hours of that late-night call: the data model was not optimized for usage.

For certain, this is an extreme case. It was highly emotional. I had never worked so hard, or been so scared, in my professional life before or since. (It is funny how FDA investigations and multimillion-dollar lawsuits can do that to you.) It is the best example of the importance of your data model and what can go wrong when you don't invest in one.

When business leaders are trying to decide whether they should invest in this thing called a data model, where the deliverable, at least from their perspective, is a drawing, I tell them this story. Data modeling is more than just a drawing of boxes and lines but provides the framework for how your organization will use the data. Now and forever, every one of my clients will be counseled on the importance of a data model.

Data modeling isn't a onetime effort. Your data and the business surrounding it changes all the time—and so should your data model. That's actually one of the hardest things about data modeling, the constant change. So in sum, it's difficult, it changes all the time, and it requires a specialized skill set. I can't emphasize the importance of data modeling enough; it is absolutely the foundation on which you build your program.

BI and IT: Frenemies

Technology and architecture is where traditional IT meets BI. These functions are really important to keeping your program running smoothly.

The IT team will be critical to the care and feeding of the environment that your end users will be accessing. If the server needs to be maintained or upgraded, or you need someone to fix the server if it crashes, this team is the team to do it.

Much of what happens in this department won't even hit the radar screen of the average BI user, and that's exactly what you want. If you don't have direct managerial responsibility for this group, it's a good idea to put some service-level agreements (SLAs) in place to ensure a timely response to issues. Some of these functions can be outsourced to your internal IT team. Examples of activities that will be managed by your IT team are:

- Supporting the BI infrastructure and processes
- Server and web administration
- Application architecture
- Metadata repository
- Application development and management
- Usage tracking
- Customer support

Part of the BI team's responsibility is to determine the level of system availability that you require. High availability means that the hardware and software are available 24 hours a day and seven days a week. If that's really what your end users expect, then that's what you request from your IT team. This decision will impact how your IT needs to support the BI deployment and will change how you write your SLAs.

Application architecture is the landscape of all the products that your organization uses that require hardware. This can include your BI products, but it can include other products as well. This team ensures that all of the applications are on stable platforms and ensure availability. This special type of architecture associated with applications ensures that the system takes the best advantage of what you have in the hardware.

ETL is the mechanism most BI efforts use to get data out of the source systems and into an integrated data warehouse. ETL is a more technical function and has impacts to both technology and architecture. More complex than a simple dump and load, which many of us do, good ETL offers us the opportunity not only to apply business rules (the *T* in *ETL*) but also introduce quality checks into the data. ETL is critically important to the success of healthcare BI programs because it's the primary and most significant opportunity we have to prepare data for usage by end users. If your team is a team full of data analysts, that's one thing, but if your intention is to improve end-user self-service, you must spend time reviewing the data, aggregating it (so that one encounter is aggregated from its original 217 rows of data), and loading it into your data model that has been created with scalability and usability in mind.

Support Calls

Whether or not you are prepared for them, support calls will happen. Users are logging into your system every day of the week, many of them from different locations. If you plan to have some level of customer support in place to manage these calls, your users will perceive a better level of service and end-user adoption will be more successful. It's unlikely that establishing a support plan alone will save a struggling BI program. If the data are "wrong" and the performance is poor, no amount of support will help you, but everything else being equal, support programs tell your end users that you are serious about making their experience with the product positive.

In your plan, create three levels of support. The nature of the call will determine how quickly you need to respond. Generally speaking, unless your BI program is driving your business, Level One calls are rare. Level One calls are the calls that require intervention within eight business hours (i.e., the same day the call is placed, e.g., when the server goes down). If your BI program really runs your business, then questionable data quality might become a Level One call. For the rest of us, that's probably a Level Two call that can be managed within two business days (or three, depending on how forgiving your end users are). Finally, Level Three calls are for reports not running, or strange fonts or spacing. Believe me, these things happen.

VALUE

A few years ago I was working with a provider organization just starting its BI program. It had purchased a BI platform and then management realized that they needed to decide where to begin using it. For this organization, the starting point was easy. It had grown through acquisition, and although that provided challenges in itself, the biggest problem was that the leaders were trying to manage the whole enterprise through a series of spreadsheets. These spreadsheets took hours and hours each month to complete. They were also error prone, as one fat-fingering mishap could cost the organization valuable time and a potentially flawed decision.

It was decided that the first spreadsheet the BI team would work to replace would be the management key performance indicators (KPIs). The KPIs had already been identified and defined. We knew where the data came from and how messy it was. All we needed to do was integrate the data from the disparate source systems and put it together in the BI interface product.

Approximately six months later we had replaced the spreadsheet with a new visually appealing dashboard. It had thresholds and gauges that indicated to management when bed days were lower than forecasted or when staffing was higher or lower than optimal. The value the dashboard provided to the organization was immeasurable. It kickstarted the entire BI program that continues today. One of the smartest moves the organization made at the outset was deciding not to boil the ocean. We picked one project that would deliver value, we created a solid foundation that provided room for growth, but we focused all of our efforts on that first deliverable.

Six months does seem like a long time to wait to produce something. But when you are just getting started, and this work is new to you and your team, six months is a reasonable expectation. Once this first big effort is done, though, development time for subsequent projects should diminish considerably.

From the "starting small" approach to the design of data, all of these factors influence the amount and perception of value. The way we define value in this context is the method and processes required to deliver information to end users to improve decision-making ability. We need to cover many aspects of value; we address a few of the key ones here.

Training

To ensure value as perceived by end users, be sure that you offer training. Although it's not usually the first thing that comes to mind when you start your BI program, it has the potential of making or breaking end-user adoption. Today's BI tools are easy to use compared to even five years ago, but that doesn't mean that users will have an easy time adapting. Even if they are used to using BI tools, a major upgrade or change to a new platform can really challenge end users. It's best to be proactive and have a thorough training program up and running the week before you go live. Don't make it any earlier than that because people will forget, and even with one week it's good to have a "sandbox" environment—a place that allows users to experience the BI platform until it goes into production.

It's important to have different delivery methods for your training program. Use products like Camtasia to create an online training program that users can log into any time to find lessons on simple tasks like logging in, changing preferences, selecting dates, and so on. Creating an online program will reduce calls to your team. Offer in-person courses frequently during the month of a release and repeat them at least once a month from then on. Create a set of printable documentation for those folks who just have to see the written word on paper. Try to remember that most of your end users will only log into the system once a month. In the meantime they have a job to do that fills up most of their memory bank. Their approach to the BI tool is like your approach to your 401(k) website; you do it when you need the data to make better decisions.

Business Analysts

Business analytics, or business analysts, are an integral part of delivering value. First, it's important to clarify what I mean by *business analysts*. Refer to Chapter 1 of *Healthcare Business Intelligence*, where we define BI;

it's clear that BI is an enablement mechanism. Therefore, you don't go to your BI group to learn about your business. Your BI group should be enabling your business teams to do that. Business analysts (BAs) are the people who document requirements from the business and translate them for consumption by IT. They are not "analysts" in the sense of analyzing data.

Data visualization is a term that probably wasn't muttered often in the average organization a few years back. Conceptually, the idea is to take the mountain of data confronting us and turn it into something that can be easily consumed visually. The advancements in BI tools in the past few years have resulted in the ability to easily produce sophisticated data visualizations. From web to mobile, making sure that your data is easily consumed is a clear way to provide value.

Now that we have a clear understanding of what BAs do, we understand that their role is particularly important and challenging. They are the bridge between technical and business. The closer you can get these two concepts together, the better off you will be. Often "requirements" get lost in translation, where business users articulate their needs in a straightforward but nonspecific way (such as "give me the data") and IT users are looking for something specific (such as where the data can be found, how it should be transformed, and the frequency with which it should be displayed). Without BAs that gap means rework, and rework means longer timelines and more money. Investing in BAs may save your organization money in the long run.

Project Management

Project management provides a methodology to manage resources and tasks toward a common end goal. Having a method for managing all of the activities involved in a BI implementation and rollout is important. The well-documented methods of good project management are what we are looking for. We need a method of planning and managing many tasks. It doesn't matter whether you subscribe to Project Management Professional methods, Project Management Institute methods, waterfall, iterative, or agile methods—that is not really at issue. Besides having a well-accepted project management method throughout your organization, you also must have a way of managing to milestones and assessing whether you are on time. Consistency with rolling out content is an important aspect of delivering value. If you are not constantly finding ways to get the job done and getting new content in the end users' hands, then you are not delivering value.

Planning

Beyond project management, you will want to do some planning in the form of roadmaps. Roadmaps are an excellent way to look out onto the landscape and plan your course for the next 18 months. This longer-term view requires a vision of what BI can provide to the organization and a path to get you there. Roadmaps should outline your BI journey. As you do this, make sure that you leave room for later modifications. That old saying about the best-laid plans applies to roadmaps as well. The real value of a roadmap is as a tool to help you articulate to supporters and dissenters alike what the program will be delivering and when.

CULTURAL IMPLICATIONS

The final tenet is the cultural implication of BI programs. Initially, I didn't make this a tenet. I've always felt that it was important, but I wasn't sure it was something that had to be addressed as a primary ingredient for success. As I got further along I recognized that although it's the most "fluffy" of all the tenets, it is the one that, after all is said and done, can make or break your program.

Change is hard, and pushing an organization from management by instinct to management by data introduces all sorts of challenges. If you understand the impact that the culture has on the change, and you have a plan to manage that change, the transition will be smoother for everyone.

In Chapter 7 we review a series of assessments that help you determine how prepared your organization is to adopt this type of change. Chapter 7 also guides you in how to tackle the results in a stepwise approach to improve your organization's ability to adapt to managing with data.

SEEKING EQUILIBRIUM

You may have noticed by now how interconnected the BI world is. One of the challenges associated with this work is trying to decide what to do when. Don't worry; we'll go into that later. But what's important to understand is that what you do has an impact on other aspects of BI. Thinking about it this way reminded me of my fourth-grade science class and the ecosystem. (See Figure B.2).

We must seek out equilibrium in all aspects of BI work. If one area in the ecosystem gets out of balance the other areas will compensate for it until it can come back inline, or one of the other areas fails. Frankly, if you were to do an analysis of the reasons why BI programs fail, 9 times out of 10 it could be traced back to a false sense of equilibrium within the ecosystem. It's important to remember from this perspective that the ecosystem in its entirety is your organization. The BI program will live and die within the confines of your organization.

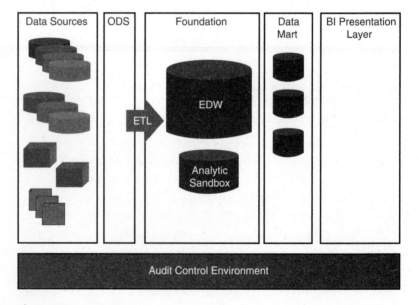

Figure B.2 BI Ecosystem

Estimating the Efforts

HOW MUCH CAN YOU DO?

The first impression you may have after the joint application design (JAD) is that there is a lot of work to do, and you're probably going to feel like you don't have the time and resources to do it all. The next step is to determine that in objective terms.

We use the SDLC model, because what we are focusing on at this point is *packets* of work. Some of that may be reports or dashboards but it may also include pilots or proof of concept (POC) work. In addition, you should estimate any programmatic features because they will require resources as well. I recommend breaking this out into buckets that are associated with the SDLC. This is helpful because it will allow you to plan the effort with parallel work paths. In other words, your analysis and design effort is usually done with your business analysts, but while they are working on another project, there's no reason that your developers can't be working on something else. Knowing this discrete type of data allows you to best align your team. It also highlights where you may have some staffing gaps, as in the table below. Although these are theoretical numbers, it's well known that the development portion of business intelligence work, including extract, transform, and load, architecture, and report/dashboard development, accounts for approximately 80 percent of the effort. Calculating the impact to your project and staff can start here.

Assessing Available Time

SDLC	Total FTE* Hours	Total Project Hours
Analysis	2,400	1,000
Design	1,600	1,000
Development	8,000	16,000
Test	2,000	1,000
Deployment	2,000	1,000

* Number of people in a role multiplied by working hours in a year (average 50 weeks)

Your timetable may look a bit different depending on the number of POCs or pilots and the amount of analysis you have to do on standardization. Regardless, you have to do this planning in some way because it's part of reducing the unknowns about the program. The more you can plan and communicate what you are doing and when you are doing it, the better off you will be. If your organization has a formal project management office, collaborate with them on this part of the work. They have the discipline that will be advantageous for you as you go forward. Don't forget to include your time as well as any time from a governance council so you can provide a complete picture to your executive sponsor.

Business Metrics

One of the key attributes of a data-driven healthcare organization (DDHO) is having a data-savvy user base. That may require some effort. This appendix is a presentation that I have used in the past to get business users thinking about data, basic descriptive statistics, and how data can be best visualized.

Applying Business Metrics to Decision Making

Slide 1. Applying Business Metrics to Decision Making

- Standards of measurement
- Trends
- Relationships
- Using data for decision making
- Being a skeptical consumer

Slide 2. Agenda

- What examples do you have that you are or have been dealing with that have been top of mind for you as we discussed these items? Was there anything that specifically brought you to this class?

Slide 3. First . . .

LET'S BEGIN WITH THE BASICS

Slide 4. Let's Begin with the Basics

- Categorical variable (often referred to as an attribute)—a variable that places an individual into one of several groups or categories.
  —Examples: Member, Benefit, Eligibility Status
- Quantitative variable (often referred to as a fact)—numerical values on which arithmetic operations are likely performed
  —Examples: Age, days inpatient, dosage of medicine, systolic blood pressure, level of calcium in the blood, etc.

Slide 5. Different Types of Variables

- Standards of Measurement

Descriptive Statistics

Slide 6. Standards of Measurement: Descriptive Statistics

Average for things like PMPM (although that's rationalized, you still create an average per month) or bed days; create a standard or baseline for measurement. In many ways we use these as attributes to other things. Most of the decisions we make in business are based on these descriptive statistics. Excel supports these and other basic statistical applications. These standards of measurement can be very informative; just don't go too far with assumptions.

- Mean: The average value of a population or set of numbers
- Median: The middle occurring value
- Mode: The most frequent occurring value
- Range & Min/Max: The maximum and minimum value, subtracted is the range
- Standard Deviation: The average occurring variance from the mean, represented as the same unit as the data (i.e., percentages or decimal points)

Slide 7. Standards of Measurement

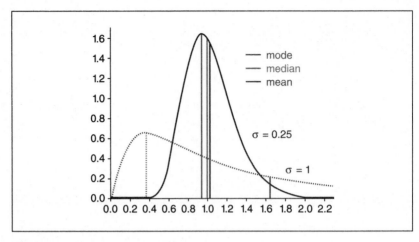

Slide 8. Measures of Central Tendency

The mean and median should be close when comparing—otherwise you run the risk of the distribution being skewed right or left. Look at the difference and assess whether it is significant and how to handle it given the context in which you're working.

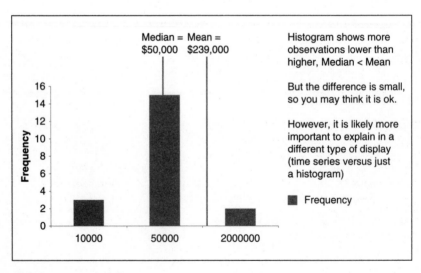

Slide 9. Mean and Median

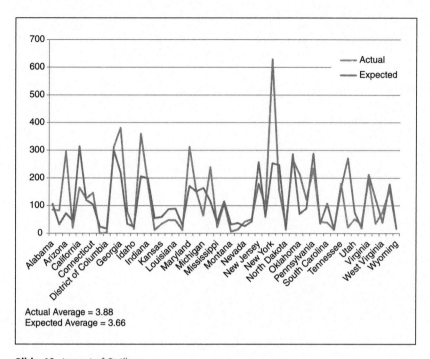

Slide 10. Impact of Outliers

- Density & Normality

Bell Curves

Slide 11. Density and Normality: Bell Curves

DENSITY CURVE

A *density curve* is a curve that: (1) is always on or above the horizontal axis, and (2) has area exactly 1 underneath it. A density curve describes the overall pattern of the distribution. The area under the curve and above any range of values is the proportion of all observations that fall in that range.

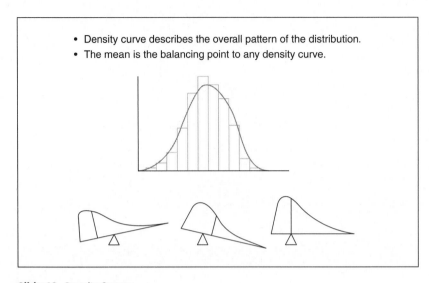

Slide 12. Density Curves
Sources: http://www.stats4stem.org/r-histograms-and-density-plots.html;
http://dept.econ.yorku.ca/~jbsmith/ec2500_1998/lecture9/Lecture9.html.

In the normal distribution with a mean of *mu* and standard deviation of *sigma*:

- 68 percent of observations fall within 1 standard deviation of the mean.
- 95 percent of the observations fall within 2 standard deviations of the mean.
- 99.7 percent of the observations fall within 3 standard deviations of the mean.

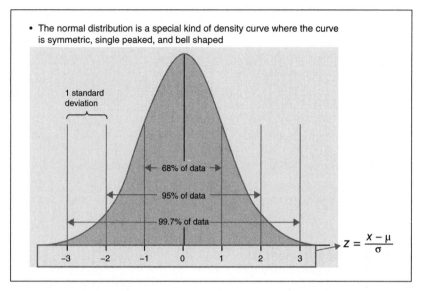

Slide 13. Normal Distribution
Source: http://faculty.virginia.edu/PullenLab/WJIIIDRBModule/WJIIIDRBModule_print.html.

Be sure that when using a *mean*, you understand the standard deviation associated with the distribution to ensure you're not introducing risk using a number such as a mean. It may be more beneficial to include quartiles or a confidence interval range, depending on the level of risk the decision is associated with.

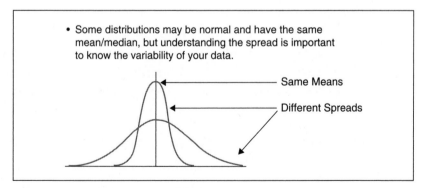

Slide 14. Data Variability in a Normal Distribution
Source: http://personal.kenyon.edu/hartlaub/MellonProject/normal2.html.

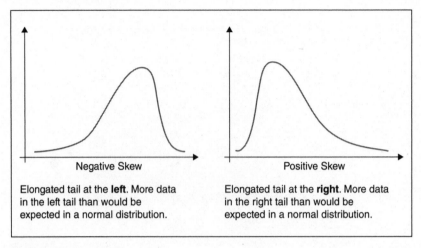

Slide 15. Skewness Left and Right
Source: http://en.wikipedia.org/wiki/Skewness.

To get Excel 2010 to produce the histogram shown in Slide 15, perform the following steps:

1. Go to File → Options → Add-Ins.
2. Under Manage (bottom of screen) click the Go . . . button.
3. Check the Analysis Toolpack and click OK.
4. When the above steps are complete, perform the following:
   ■ Go to the Data Ribbon.
   ■ Click on Data Analysis.
   ■ Answer the prompts. Input Range will be your quantitative variable; you don't need a BIN—that will be created for you—click labels if you included a label in your histogram, and click the Chart Output checkbox to show the chart that you see above.

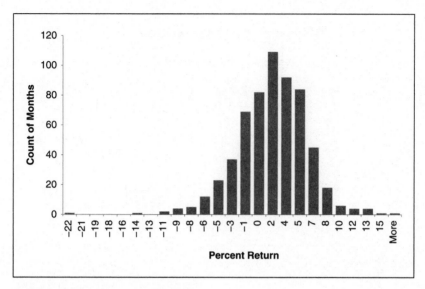

Slide 16. Which Skew Is This Distribution?

- Best practices for viewing certain variable types:
  —Categorical Variables
  - Bar Graphs
  - Pie Charts
  - Pareto Chart
  —Quantitative Variables
  - Histogram
  - Time Plots
  —Combination: Using both categorical and quantitative
  - Boxplots

Slide 17. Examining a Distribution

The number of variables should be visibly manageable. If there are too many, it can be too hard to differentiate what's important or relevant. Limit the selection to the top 10 or 20.

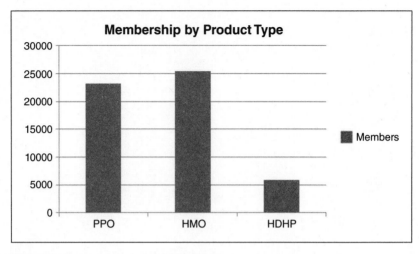

Slide 18. Viewing Categorical Variables Bar Chart

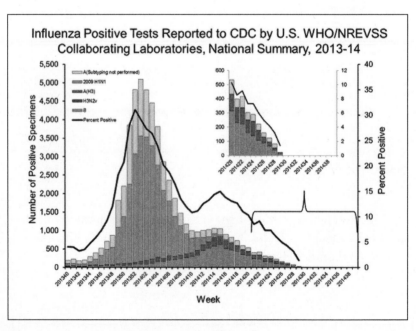

Slide 19. Viewing Categorical Variables Combination Chart
Source: http://www.cdc.gov/flu/weekly/?mobile=nocontent

The purpose of this graph is to understand the data. The groupings are not important. We went with whole numbers (1–2, 2–3, etc.) where you could easily do the same thing using 0.5 precision or others depending on your software program. Make sure to understand that the pattern of the data seems to resemble what's called a *normal distribution*—the foundation of much of the statistical analysis that is performed in business today.

EXAMINING DISTRIBUTIONS

In any graph of data, look for the overall pattern and for striking deviations from that pattern. You can describe the overall pattern of a histogram by its shape, center, and spread. An important kind of deviation is an *outlier*, an individual value that falls outside the overall pattern.

Concepts of Symmetric and Skewed Distributions

- *Symmetric:* The left and right sides of the histogram are approximately mirror images of one another.
- *Skewed to the right* (different than you may think): The right side of the histogram (containing the half of the observations with larger values) extends much farther than the left side.
- *Skewed to the left* (different than you may think): The left side of the histogram extends much farther out than the right side.

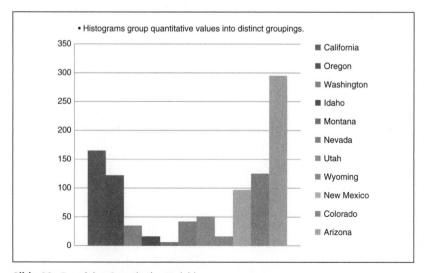

Slide 20. Examining Quantitative Variables

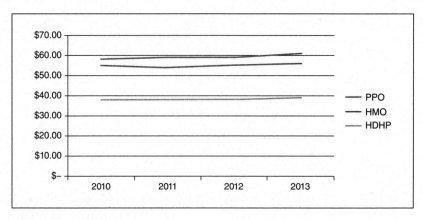

Slide 21. Time Plots

The five-number summary of a distribution consists of the smallest observation, the first quartile, the median, the third quartile, and the largest observation, written in order from smallest to largest.

- A boxplot is a graph of the five-number summary.
- A central box spans the quartiles.
- A line in the box marks the median.
- Lines extend from the box out to the smallest and largest observations.

Boxplots are most useful for side-by-side comparison of several distributions (quantitative variable grouped by a qualitative variable).

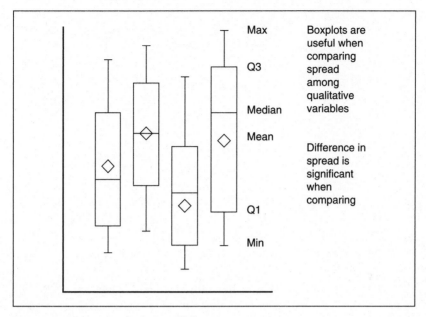

Slide 22. Five-Number Summary and Boxplots
Source: SAS Institute.

In your small groups, answer this question:

- What implications are there if you understood the descriptive statistics associated with any of these populations?

Slide 23. Exercise 1

- What are they and how can we use them?

Trends

Slide 24. Trends: What Are They and How Can We Use Them?

- Key element of trend is TIME.
- Trends are meant to be an indicator of the FUTURE
- Not all trends are helpful

"The best predictor of future behavior is past behavior".
—Mark Twain

Slide 25. Attributes of Trends

NOTE:

The *trendline* for the data series looks to be increasing, even though the end of the time series shows a significant decline. This is a deception that can happen when generalizing a trend off a long time series of data, not taking into account recent events that may cause a shift in the overall behavior of the individuals.

ANOTHER NOTE:

Information typically is reported as *seasonally adjusted* to take out the peaks and valleys so recipients know how much above/below normal the index is.

A *time plot* of a variable plots each observation against the time at which it was measured. Always put time on the horizontal scale of your plot and the variable you are measuring on the vertical scale. Connecting the data points by lines helps emphasize any change over time.

A pattern in a time series that repeats itself at known regular intervals of time is called *seasonal variation*.

A *trend* in a time series is a persistent, long-time rise or fall.

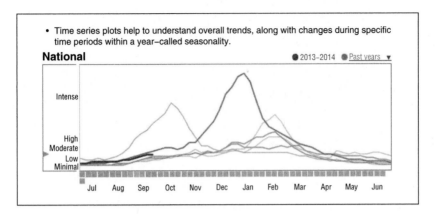

Slide 26. Quantitative Variable Trend Plot

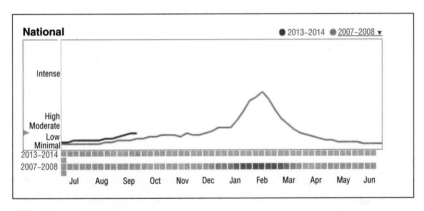

Slide 27. Predicting Trends

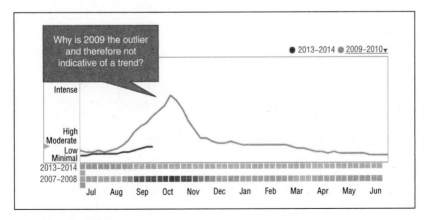

Slide 28. An Outlier

- Step 1: Arrange the observations in increasing order and locate the median in the ordered list of observations.
- Step 2: The first quartile is the median of the observations whose position in the ordered list is to the left of the location of the overall median.
- Step 3: The third quartile is the median of the observations whose position in the ordered list is to the right of the location of the overall median.

Slide 29. Measuring Spread of Your Data Using Quartile

- Causation and Regression

Examining relationships between variables

Slide 30. Causation and Regression: Examining Relationships between Variables

One of the most common errors we find in the press is the confusion between *correlation* and *causation* in scientific and health-related studies. In theory, these are easy to distinguish—an action or occurrence can *cause* another (such as smoking causes lung cancer), or it can *correlate* with another (such as smoking is correlated with alcoholism). If one action causes another, then they are most certainly correlated. But just because two things occur together does not mean that one caused the other, even if it seems to make sense.

- In general, it is extremely difficult to establish causality between two correlated events or observances.
- Smoking and alcoholism
- Day-time TV and eating disorders
- http://www.stats.org/faq_vs.htm

- In contrast, there are many statistical tools to establish a statistically significant correlation.

Slide 31. Causality versus Correlation

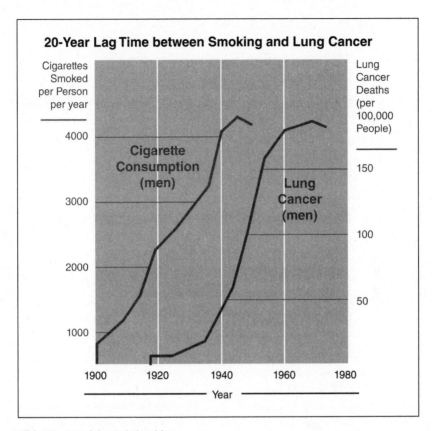

Slide 32. Examining Relationships

Facts about Correlation and What You Need to Know to Interpret Correlation

- Correlation makes no distinction between explanatory and response variables. It makes no difference which variable you call *x* and which you call *y* in calculating the correlation.
- Correlation requires that both variables be quantitative, so that it makes sense to do the arithmetic indicated by the formula for *r*.
- Because *r* uses the standardized values of the observations, *r* does not change when we change the units of measurement of x, *y*, or both.

- Positive *r* indicates positive association between the variables, and negative *r* indicates negative association.

- The correlation *r* is always a number between −1 and 1. Values of *r* near 0 indicate a very weak linear relationship. The strength of the linear relationship increases as *r* moves away from 0 toward either −1 or 1.

- Correlation measures the strength of only a linear relationship between two variables—not curved relationships. One would need to straighten out the values to perform a correlation if required.

- Like the mean and standard deviation, the correlation is not resistant: *r* is strongly affected by a few outlying observations.

Correlation is not a complete description of two-variable data, even when the relationship between the variables is linear. Make sure you include the means and standard deviations for context of the correlation and how much cause and effect exists.

- Correlation measures two things; strength and direction (negative or positive).
- The closer the one (1) the correlation is, the more related the two quantitative variables are.

Strong Positive

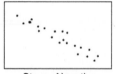
Strong Negative

Week Positive

Slide 33. Correlations
Source: http://blog.simplilearn.com/quality-management/correlation-part-1.

- When viewing data that looks related, avoid jumping to causation (even if it seems obvious)
- Statistically, there are ways to determine causation versus relation . . . but only statistically
- Why would we care about the difference between causality & correlation for everyday business decisions?

Slide 34. Avoid the Easy Answer

In your small groups, answer this question:

- What can you ascertain from this trend? What information do you have? What information is not available?

Slide 35. Exercise 2

- Being a Skeptical Consumer

Pitfalls of graphs

Slide 36. Being a Skeptical Consumer: Pitfalls of Graphs

- Darrell Huff, *How to Lie with Statistics*, Penguin Books, 1973
- Edward Tufte, *Envisioning Information, The Quantitative Display of Information & Beautiful Evidence*, Graphics Press, 1990, 1996, 2002
- Stephen Few, *Now You See It: Simple Visualization Techniques for Quantitative Analysis*, Analytics Press, 2009

Slide 37. Excellent Resources

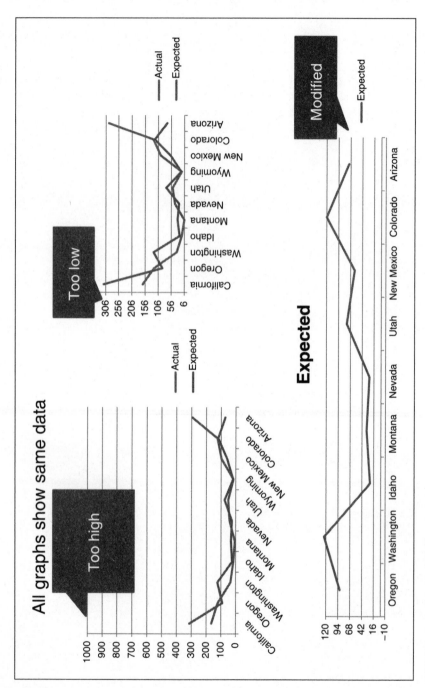

Slide 38. Importance of Scale

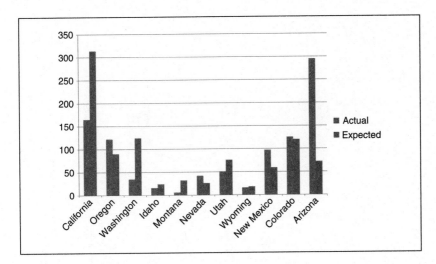

Slide 39. Rigging the Scale

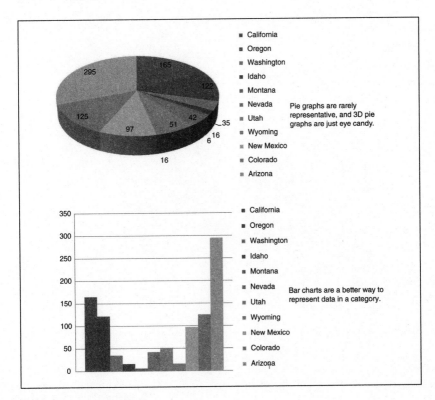

Slide 40. A Perfect 100?

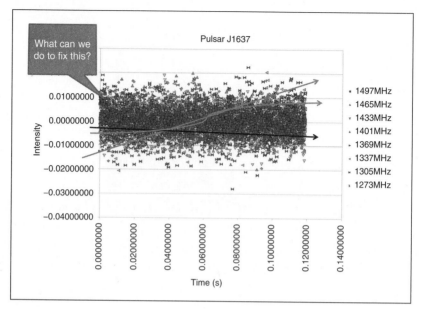

Slide 41. Noisy Data

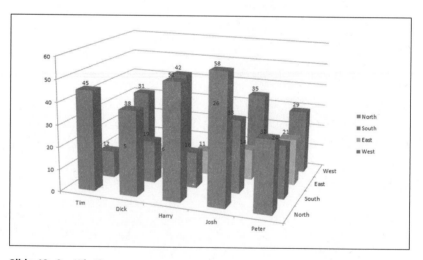

Slide 42. Say *What?*

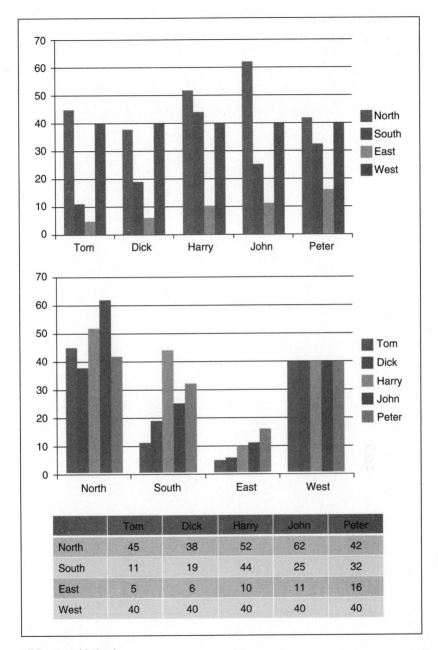

	Tom	Dick	Harry	John	Peter
North	45	38	52	62	42
South	11	19	44	25	32
East	5	6	10	11	16
West	40	40	40	40	40

Slide 43. Said Clearly

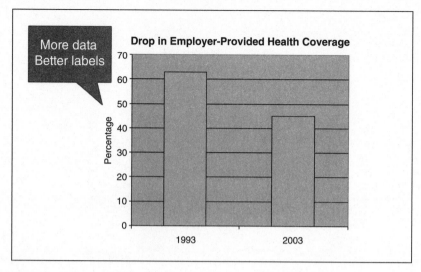

Slide 44. And You Are . . .

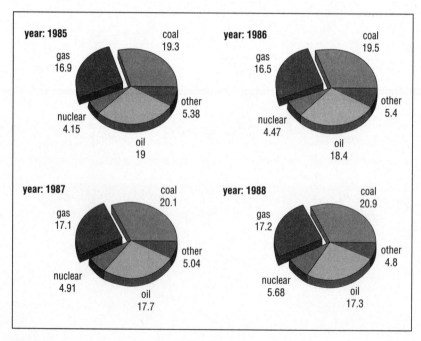

Slide 45. You Can't Represent a Trend with a Pie Graph

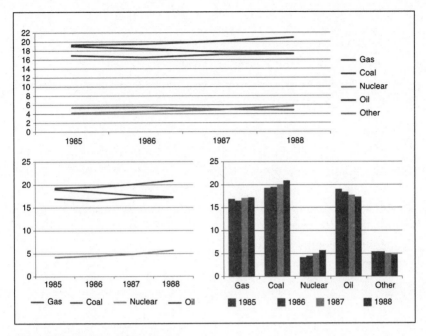

Slide 46. Same Data, Better Visuals

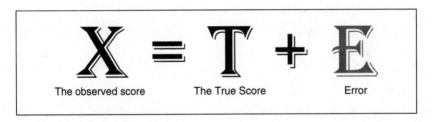

Slide 47. Rule of Applied Analytics

In your small groups, answer this question:

• How can you apply the things we discussed today to your job? Is there anything you will do or think about differently?

Slide 48. Exercise 3

Appendix

Additional Content

Slide 49. Appendix: Additional Content

To find the *mean* of a set of observations, add their values and divide by the number of observations. This is one of the most common measures of center—even though it comes with its pitfalls. Mention the need to understand the histogram and the normal distribution before making any assessments of how valid the mean is in relation to the decision needing to be made.

Median: Half of the observations are above and half of the observations are below this value. The purest (nonparametric, or not needing a normal distribution) form of the middle. Additional calculations are performed if there are an even number of observations (or individuals), but either way it's a 50/50 shot when calculating the median: 50 above and 50 below the value.

Note: Confidence intervals won't be covered in this course, but it's a good measure of how far from the mean we can go given the distribution being analyzed.

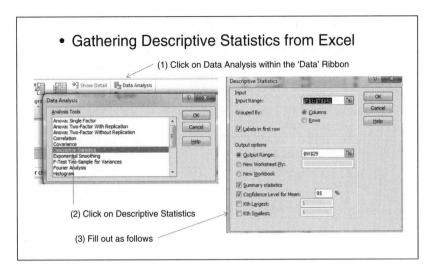

Slide 50. Measuring Center: Mean and Median

Column1	
Mean	239000
Standard Error	134706.1129
Median	50000
Mode	50000
Standard Deviation	602424.0507
Sample Variance	3.62915E+11
Kurtosis	7.025321872
Skewness	2.884769913
Range	1990000
Minimum	10000
Maximum	2000000
Sum	4780000
Count	20

Slide 51. Output from Excel

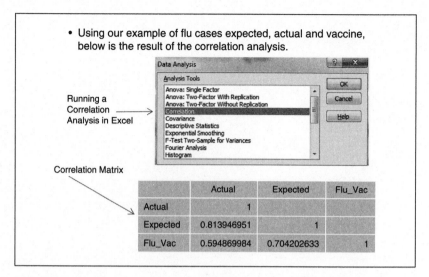

Slide 52. Performing a Correlation Analysis

Food prices can be shown to trend almost any way you like—just pick a few items to influence the conclusion.

■ Avocados—cheaper than ever!

■ Milk—prices are lower when bought at the gas station.

Watch for samples that cherry-pick the data to prove a forgone conclusion.

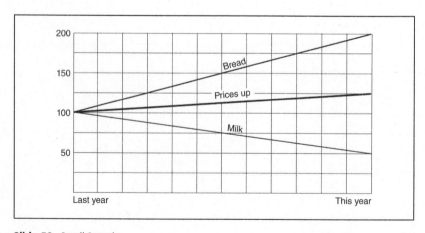

Slide 53. Small Sample

A *response variable* measures an outcome of a study. These variables are also referred to as *dependent variables*.

An *explanatory variable* explains or influences changes in a response variable. These variables are also referred to as *independent variables*.

EXAMINING A SCATTERPLOT

In any graph of data, look for the overall pattern and for striking deviations from the pattern.

You can describe the overall pattern of a scatterplot by the form, direction, and strength of the relationship. *Form* is the pattern—linear, exponential, polynomial; *direction* is determining the positive or negative association between the variables; *strength* is determined by how closely the points follow a clear form.

Two variables are *positively associated* when above-average values of one tend to accompany above-average values of the other and below-average values also tend to occur together.

Two variables are *negatively associated* when above-average values of one tend to accompany below-average values of the other, and vice versa.

An important kind of deviation is an *outlier*, an individual value that falls outside the overall pattern of the relationship.

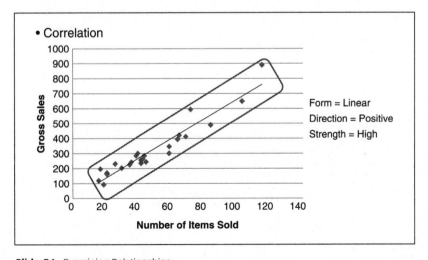

Slide 54. Examining Relationships

Agenda | Company Name | JAD Session

JAD Session Objective:
The purpose of this Requirements Workshop is to accurately define the requirements/scope and roadmap strategy for ad hoc reporting to be delivered within the project.

Day, Date

Start Time

Activities	Duration	Comments
Introduction	30 minutes (9:30)	Quick round robin introductions.
Ground Rules	30 minutes (10:00)	Define ground rules for all of us to abide by during our time together.
Definitions	30 minutes (10:30)	What does ad hoc mean? How will it look and feel in the business intelligence (BI) environment?
Break	15 minutes (10:45)	
Business Process Discussion	30 minutes (11:15)	Income Statement
Small-Group Breakout	45 minutes (12:00)	Consider the things that you attempt to solve for every day with data. Make sure to represent these statements in business terms. Write these down so that the statement reflects the guidelines of ad hoc that have been established.
Lunch	45 minutes (12:45)	
Group Discussion	30 minutes (1:15)	How have your ad hoc statements changed or not changed?
Business Process Discussion	30 minutes (1:45)	Balance Sheet
Break	15 minutes (2:00)	
Small-Group Breakout	45 minutes (2:45)	Discuss balance sheet/inventory and other business statements that haven't been vetted.
Group Discussion	45 minutes (3:30)	Discuss the business cases; discuss the results of the day. What questions/concerns?

Day, Date, Departure Time

170

Activities	Duration	Comments
Discuss Current State Recommendations	30 minutes (9:30)	At the end of the discussion yesterday, where did we end up? What issues were presenting themselves? Did anyone have an epiphany overnight?
Data Analysis Considerations	1 hour (10:30)	What would be interesting to see this data by? (i.e., how many customers in a particular sub-set of products)
Break	15 minutes (10:45)	
Small-Group Breakout	30 minutes (11:15)	Discuss the ad hoc statements we have prioritized and see what business questions you could answer with this data. What questions can't you answer? What's missing?
Group Discussion	30 minutes (11:45)	What did you find in the small-group breakout?
Review Roadmap and 'What's Missing; Review Parking Lot.	15 minutes (12:00)	

We will do our best to stick as close to the agenda as possible in regard to time. We may find that the conversation changes organically and that brings us to an area that is critical to explore. If that happens, we will go with it, which may mean that we will not do a group breakout or will delay the specific topic associated with a group discussion. That's okay as long as it is aligned with our objective for the session.

Data Visualization Guide

T his appendix will provide you with a starting template to create your own data visualization guide. The text is provided; you complete it by including your organization's branding, color palette, and sample graphs.

PURPOSE OF THIS DOCUMENT

Your organization's goal is to become a data-driven healthcare organization. *Data-driven* means that information must be consumable and contextual, to encourage action that will modify behavior over time. This guide provides developers of dashboards with a set of standards for your organization to ensure a consistent and compelling work product. There are too many visuals to reference in this document, but it's important to keep in mind who your audience is. Not all visuals are created equal, and in most cases simple is better than complex. Remember, most users will not be able to consume more than three variables at a time, and time itself is a variable. That's why complex boxplots and heatmaps are not recommended in most data visualization situations.

SECTION ONE: YOUR ORGANIZATION BRAND REQUIREMENTS

Primary Color Palette

All listed in RGB

Secondary Color Palette

Opacity Options (if applicable)

EXAMINING DISTRIBUTIONS

The distribution of a variable tells what values it takes and how often it takes these values. Any good visualization of data requires context of the data, so be conscientious of what you are displaying and why.

- Categorical Variables
- Bar Graphs
- Pie Graphs
- Pareto Chart
- Quantitative Variables
- Histogram
- Stemplots
- Time Plots
- Combination
- Boxplots

Categorical Variable—represents a variable that places an individual data point into one of several groups or categories.

Examples: Medical Device Vendor, name of product, Gender of Patient, etc.

Quantitative Variable—numerical values on which arithmetic operations are likely performed (sum, average, maximum, and minimum)

Examples: Age, days in patient, dosage of medicine, systolic blood pressure, level of calcium in the blood, etc.

When to Use Bar Graphs

Your data must be categorical. In addition you must have a range that will display how the data points are related to one another. This point is tricky because in some cases you may see very little differentiation or a lot of differentiation among the individual bars, which can mislead the reader. Distortion from the *Y* axis can make the difference between two bars exaggerated. Finally, you should have no more than 12 bars to keep the graph clean.

Bar Graphs Rules:

Always use a title.

Legends are required if the data being represented is more than two categorical variables (should NOT exceed three)

The maximum of the *Y* axis should be no more than 3 percent higher than the highest occurring value.

Always follow the brand rules as established in section one of this document.

Never use 3D versions they skew the visual.

If the variation between the data points is 10 percent or less, keep the major gridlines at 5.0. If the variation is between 10 and 50 percent, go to 10.0 gridline separation. If it's above 50 percent, you can go to 15.0 but consider what data you are visualizing. There may be a better way to demonstrate that kind of variability.

When to Use a Pie Graph

Your data must be categorical. In addition, you must be representing a finite population (that represents eight or fewer data points and always equals 100 percent). *The use of pie graphs is not encouraged; use them sparingly.*

Pie Graph Rules:

Always use a title.

Legends are required.

The data being represented should not exceed 10 categorical variables.

Always follow the brand rules as established in section one of this document.

Never use the 3D version.

When to Use Pareto Charts

Pareto charts look very similar to bar graphs with one important distinction; they sort the data from largest to smallest, left to right. This helps the user compare variability between each data point. You will note that this is the same data from the bar graph, but rather than sorted alphabetically it's sorted by highest bed days. April was our highest bed-day month. Similar rules apply to bar and Pareto charts.

Pareto Chart Rules:

Always use a title.

Pareto charts should only ever represent one data point.

The maximum of the Y axis should be no more than 3 percent higher than the highest occurring value.

Always follow the brand rules as established in section one of this document

Never use the 3D version; it skews the visual.

If the variation between the data points is 10 percent or less, keep the major gridlines at 5.0. If the variation is between 10 and 50 percent, go to 10.0 gridline separation. If it's above 50 percent, you can go to 15.0 but consider what data you are visualizing. There may be a better way to demonstrate that kind of variability.

When to Use a Histogram

Histograms group quantitative values into distinct groupings. In any graph, but in histograms in particular, look for the overall pattern and striking deviations from that pattern. You can describe the overall pattern of a in histogram by its shape, center, and spread. The curvature of the histogram is informative, as is the width of the bars. An important kind of deviation is an outlier, an individual value that falls outside the overall pattern. In order to use a histogram, you must have quantitative data that can be presented in ranges, for example, frequency of bed days.

Histogram Chart Rules:

Always use a title.

The maximum of the Y axis should be no more than 3 percent higher than the highest occurring value.

Always follow the brand rules as established in section one of this document

Never use the 3D version; it skews the visual.

When to Use a Time Plot or Line Graph

Your data must be quantitative to use a time plot. Always put time on the horizontal scale of your plot and the variable you are measuring on the vertical scale. Connecting the data points by lines helps emphasize any change over time. In order to truly demonstrate a trend, you must have three years of data. Line graphs are often used with less data than that, but be wary of trends from them. When plotting a line graph, you should have be representing no more than eight categories. It's important to keep the graph very clean to ensure clarity of the message.

Line Graphs Rules:

Always use a title.

Legends are required if the data being represented is more than one categorical variable (should NOT exceed eight).

The maximum of the Y axis should be no more than 3 percent higher than the highest occurring value. It should always start at zero.

Always follow the brand rules as established in section one of this document

Never use the 3D version; it skews the visual.

Ensure that there is separation between lines to ensure clarity. If the lines are very similar, always use symbols to differentiate the lines.

When to Use a Combination Graph

A combination graph can be shown either as a bar or a line graph, and it includes a goal, target, or threshold line. Your data must be quantitative. Generally, because you are demonstrating a goal and goals are typically set for one year, the data is for one year. It's important to keep the graph very clean to ensure clarity of the message. When you are showing more than one category, you should also use symbols to differentiate the lines, in case it is printed in black and white or for the color blind.

Combination Chart Rules:

Always use a title.

Legends are required if the data being represented is more than one categorical variable (should NOT exceed eight for lines and three for bars).

Follow either the line or bar graph rules.

Always follow the brand rules as established in section one of this document

Never use the 3D version; it skews the visual.

Other graphs that show target or trends when data has variable ranges are bullet graphs.

EXAMINING RELATIONSHIPS

The relationship of variables tells what values are related, generally over time. Appropriate visualizations of correlations (method of determining the strength and direction of a relationship) require you to show the variables together, and how they change over time.

- Scatterplots
- Line graphs (same as above)
- Heatmaps

There are other ways to use the concept of a scatterplot that add more visual interest; the variations on scatterplots simply show how related two variables are to one another. As in the examples above, showing the strength (how close the dots are) and the direction (positive or negative) of the correlation is key. An example of a positive correlation would be the more you talk on the phone, the higher your phone bill.

An example of a negative correlation is the more you exercise, the less you weigh.

Scatterplot Rules:

Always use a title.

Legends are required.

Always follow the brand rules as established in section one of this document

Never use the 3D version; it skews the visual.

Afterword

Much of what I have written about in both of my books were my lessons learned as a consultant. I'd spent one-third of my professional life guiding sometimes three or four organizations at a time through the journey of business intelligence (BI). It was an exhilarating time to be a consultant, although it didn't start that way. In 2008 as the beginning of the great recession sank its teeth in, I left a large stable company to go to a small consulting firm. At the time it felt terrifying. I lost a lot of sleep those first 18 months, and it wasn't just because I had a baby at home. But then the Affordable Care Act was passed and healthcare executives realized that they had been ignoring a great asset. I'm sure that as the years pass and I look back on that time, I will consider it to be an incredible gift to be doing what I was doing at that time in history.

But all great partnerships must come to an end. The truth was, even though I was doing what I wanted to be doing professionally. it was taking an incredible toll on my family. I had a friend share with me once the anecdote about juggling balls; some of them are rubber and some are glass. The balls for your career and other commitments are made of rubber and bounce when you drop them (although not always the way you want), but the balls that are made of glass are the ones marked family and friends. If you drop those you can never put them back together again. I was dangerously close to dropping one of those glass balls. It was time to make a change.

I was fortunate once again to have impeccable timing. As I was starting the process to make this change, the one organization that had been on the top of my list since that fateful day in November 2006 was looking to hire someone for their business intelligence work. I have been given an opportunity to give back to the organization that saved my nephew's life, and countless others. I am now working at Children's Hospitals and Clinics of Minnesota.

As I write these words, I am starting my fourth week as an employee and not a consultant. In some respects it's a bit hard to shake off the "consultant" perspective because I've started a hundred new jobs in the last five years. But this time I have an actual desk, with my name on it. I've gained a new perspective for the work, the one of ownership.

The importance of ownership was never lost on me as a consultant. Whenever I worked with an organization, one of the things I stressed very early on (sometimes before they even hired me) was that I couldn't own it, they had to. I was happy to be the person behind the curtain, but they had to learn fast and take it from the baton pass (sorry, that was a lot of analogies). Now I am the one that's in front of the curtain, baton in hand. I'm ready.

As I look back on these pages and what I wrote, there is very little I would change. There is plenty I would add given the time. First, the idea of "Big Data" or what I rephrase as Diverse-Persistent Data (DPD). As you read that chapter, I'm certain my skepticism was thinly veiled. I've still not seen it in action but I now feel the pressure real time from anxious business users who just don't have access to the data that they need to do their jobs to the best of their ability. It's a by-product of long-held data warehouse best practices and the rapid change in an industry that hasn't seen that in a long time. I've been thinking nonstop about how I can feed this insatiable beast without getting eaten myself.

Recently, I've had to start commuting. I don't care for driving. It's a non-value add activity and I don't have time for such frivolity. But I've had some time to think. I like to drive fast; I have a fast car. But no matter how fast I drive there's always someone willing to go faster, sometimes WAY faster. At first I got upset. What were they thinking? It's dangerous and dumb, plus they passed me and that's just not okay! So I tried for a couple days to keep up, but I just couldn't do it. It felt wrong, traveling 80+ miles an hour on a busy morning freeway. Then I realized something; those fast drivers are like our business users. They don't care about the work that it requires to get data into a system for appropriate usage any more than those drivers care about the speed limit.

The trouble is, without a good infrastructure and police to stop the really stupid stuff, gridlock is inevitable. That's where we are at. Our infrastructure is not set up to accommodate all this activity and in many cases our police force has either gone rogue and is pulling everyone over or just gave up all together. In either case, their critical role has hindered the movement of traffic.

In order to get really good at something, you have to do it over and over. That's why when you need surgery you will generally seek out a specialist. I'm all for people learning, but if it's really serious I want the physician that's done it a thousand times. If you really want to get your data in, scalable and reliable, don't go to the guy that's created an access database. It's unstable and unreliable and it's certainly not an enterprise capability. Go to the team that can support you with enterprise tools. Admittedly, here's where we have run into an issue in the past and why I've almost always recommended that BI sits in business. It's because most technical resources will tell you all the reasons why what you want won't work. So, they act like those rogue cops and stop everything from happening, fearful of the mess that they will have to pick up if they don't. But, left alone to their own devices, the business will act the opposite and be like the cops that just give up. Either way, you end up in the same position: gridlock.

After seeing this first-hand, and now being accountable for it, it's reinforced my commitment to the hub-and-spoke model of organizational structure that I talk about in Chapter 5. Although it looks similar, the hub-and-spoke model is not a center of excellence. It may be a center for best practice, but the real goal of the hub and spoke is to take advantage of the expertise where it's at. Most data warehouse departments are really good at getting data out of applications and preparing it for usage. But they don't like understand the business context as well as the business users do. I know a lot of IT resources will argue that point; I've seen it over and over again. But the truth is your day-to-day job is very different from that of a business person. You live and breathe systems, machines, and methods. Our business users live and breathe our patients, clinical operations, and finances. Let the data warehouse team do what they are good at in the hub, getting that data in as quickly as possible, and let the business do what their best at, applying the business context. If you do that and ensure that there is constant movement between the hub and spoke (by definition), then you will be able to do incredible things very fast. That's exactly what I am going to do.

Next, we have to tackle the data itself; never an easy task. As I discussed in Chapter 3, there are so many standards and codes, just trying to marry the acute, ambulatory, and financial perspectives of the data is mind-boggling. As I plan out the next year of our new BI and analytics program here, one thing I plan to do is find some use cases for DPD. When you start anything new, it's best to start small and see where it takes you. Pulling some of the data that we have access to, such as the ambulatory or financial data, into a data lake so that we can do some data exploration before modeling may be the way to go. After doing a lot of research on DPD, I plan to dive in cautiously. Listening to the venerable Ralph Kimball this week in a webinar, I realized that there are ways to take advantage of all of what we have learned in data warehousing but still taking advantage of some exciting changes in the industry. This doesn't really change the fact that we have a standards and interoperability issue in healthcare, but I can't solve that. I can, however, solve my organization's problem of lack of access to data.

I have been charged with increasing self-service of the BI platform. I'm wary of the concept of self-service; I think it many cases it may be a fool's errand. I'm not alone in that assessment; I've had this conversation with Wayne Eckerson, a well-known data warehouse expert. Here's what I am certain about with self-service: All it does is take the pressure off of one place and put it on another. As you begin to tackle these issues, don't think that it will solve your problems, it will just put them in a new place. The very astute BI professional will plan for this. The first step in any self-service journey is to provide a highly visual method of consuming information: a dashboard. But you can't stop there; you have to give users the ability to interact with that dashboard. Then you should give savvy business users the ability to create their own. The barrier to that in the past is the concern that users will create wrong assumptions or just bad dashboards. Of course, you have to connect your dashboard tool to data you trust. Speaking of trust, you have to trust your users. If you don't, create a data visualization guidebook (Appendix F if you need a starter). This text will help users know what graphs are appropriate for different types of data and the best practices for using them. For example, I have this thing about pie graphs. Pies are okay; I currently have five in my refrigerator for my husband's birthday party this weekend. Pie graphs are not okay. They are almost never done correctly. In my data visualization guide, I tell people how to use pie graphs (you are categorizing), and when not to use pie graphs (trending data, when looking at the high/low aspects of data). I also tell people that piegraphs shouldn't be used when you have more than eight categories and then I show what colors to use based on our branding. I do that with every primary visual (bar graphs, line charts, Pareto, histogram, etc.). Perhaps it seems like overkill, but one day very soon that guidebook will save my team lots of work.

> *Freedom is actually a bigger game than power. Power is about what you can control. Freedom is about what you can unleash.*
>
> —Harriet Rubin

That will solve the "easy" stuff, the questions that any organization should be able to answer (i.e., daily census). But then your users will start asking more astute questions at a faster pace. It's like a balloon. You can push the air around but it still has the same amount of air. In many cases, the increase in self-service capabilities will increase your need, introducing more air into that balloon. Without a plan to manage that, it will pop. You will never be able to scale your BI team to meet the needs of your entire organization. The size alone will introduce too many barriers, requiring you to slow down, and nothing spells disaster like a bureaucratic BI team. You need to be small and agile to respond to the needs. An easy way to manage that is to have the analysts in the business departments do what they need to do. You give them the tools, training, and data but they stay in the business. Let them deliver to their business users and bring back to the hub new lessons learned and methods. It is self-service, but the best kind: the kind that allows you to scale while not introducing barriers.

The research that I completed for this book has helped me a great deal in facing my new challenge. I've realized that even though I've never left BI, having ownership over a program at a hospital is very different than it was six years ago, the last time I did it as an employee. My pessimistic perspective prevented me from enabling business users.

I was usually the first one to say no. But I've realized that there is no saying no anymore, because if you do, people find a way around you and you still have to clean up the mess. It's time to let them go, with good standards in place, policies and procedures for usage, and a firm understanding that there will be errors, bumps and detours. Instead of spending your time trying to get in front of these things, you have to spend your time reassessing the effort and process mapping where things failed.

I'm thrilled that I have an opportunity to practice what I've now written about. I've learned so much about the business intelligence/data warehousing industry in the last six months that I'm excited to try in practice, knowing that if it fails, I just have to try another way—because the worst thing is not trying at all.

About the Author

Laura Madsen is the author of the book *Healthcare Business Intelligence: A Guide to Empowering Successful Data Reporting and Analytics* (John Wiley & Sons, 2012). Laura has 15 years of experience in BI and data warehousing for healthcare as well as a passion for engaging and educating the BI community.

Laura leads the Enterprise BI and Analytics Program at Children's Hospitals and Clinics of Minnesota. At Children's she is charged with creating a data-driven healthcare organization. During her career, she has initiated and supported countless BI initiatives and worked with more than 50 health plans. Prior to joining Children's, Laura spent over five years as a consultant, providing guidance and advice to a multitude of healthcare organizations across the country. She has held senior positions with several leading healthcare technology companies, including UnitedHealth Group, and a national pharmacy benefit management company. During her tenure, her responsibilities included leading an enterprise BI project from pre-concept to execution, managing a commercially available suite of BI tools, and advising both business and IT leaders on effective healthcare BI practices.

In 2006 Laura co-founded the Twin Cities chapter of The Data Warehouse Institute (TDWI), and in 2008 she founded the Healthcare BI Summit. Laura gives talks nationally and internationally about the importance and power of data in healthcare.

Index